This Book Bel[illegible]gs To

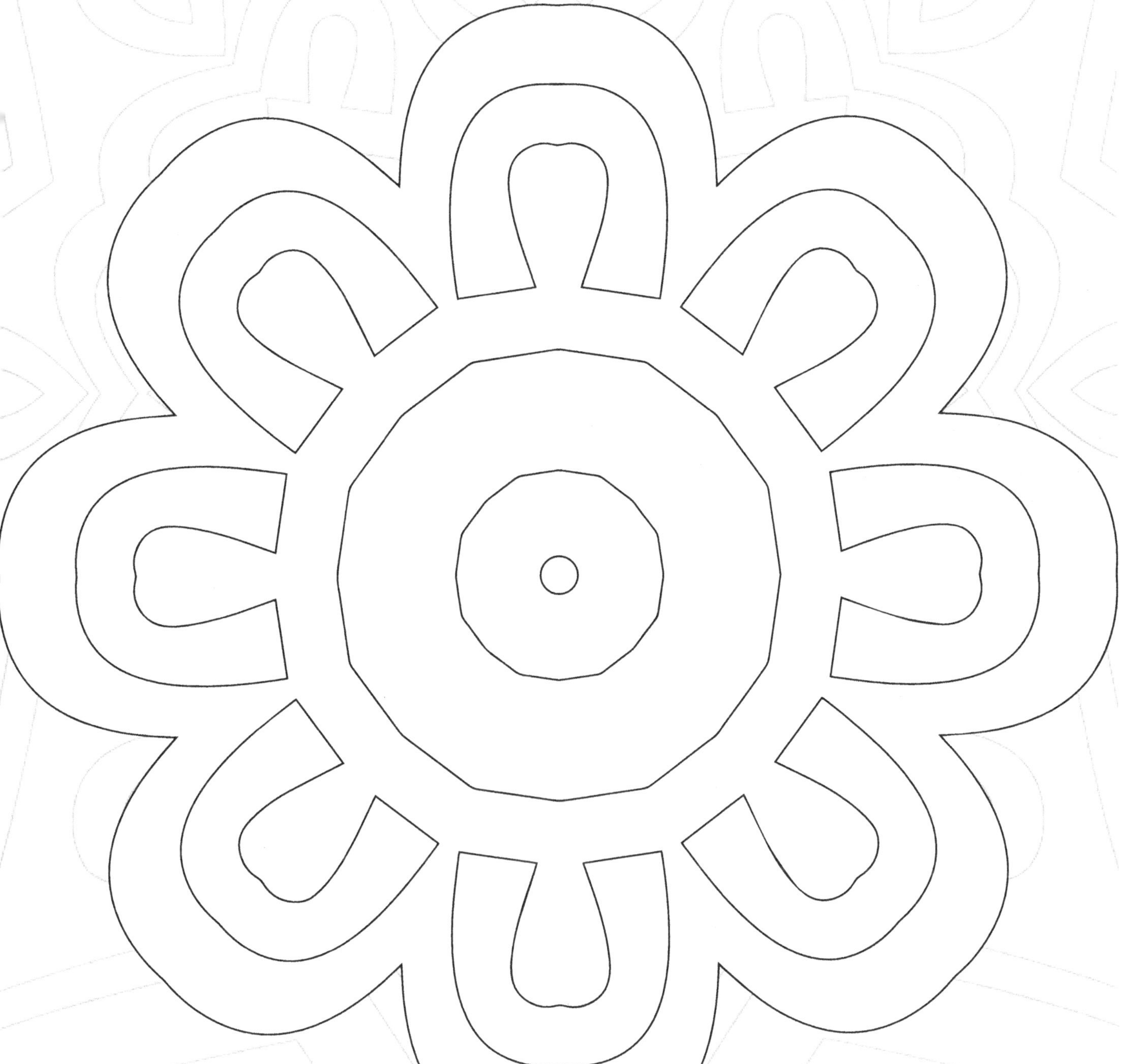

Coloring Test Page

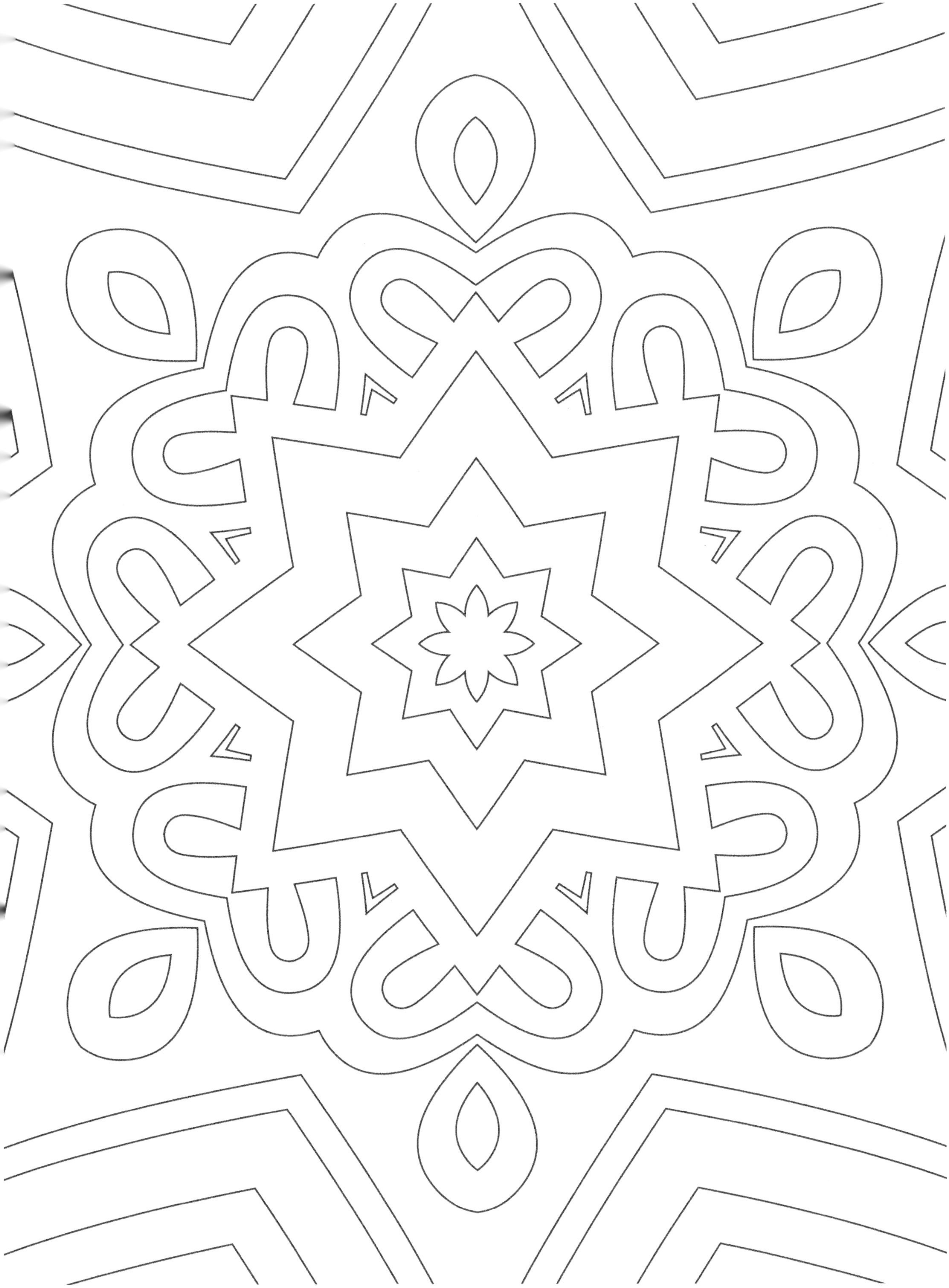

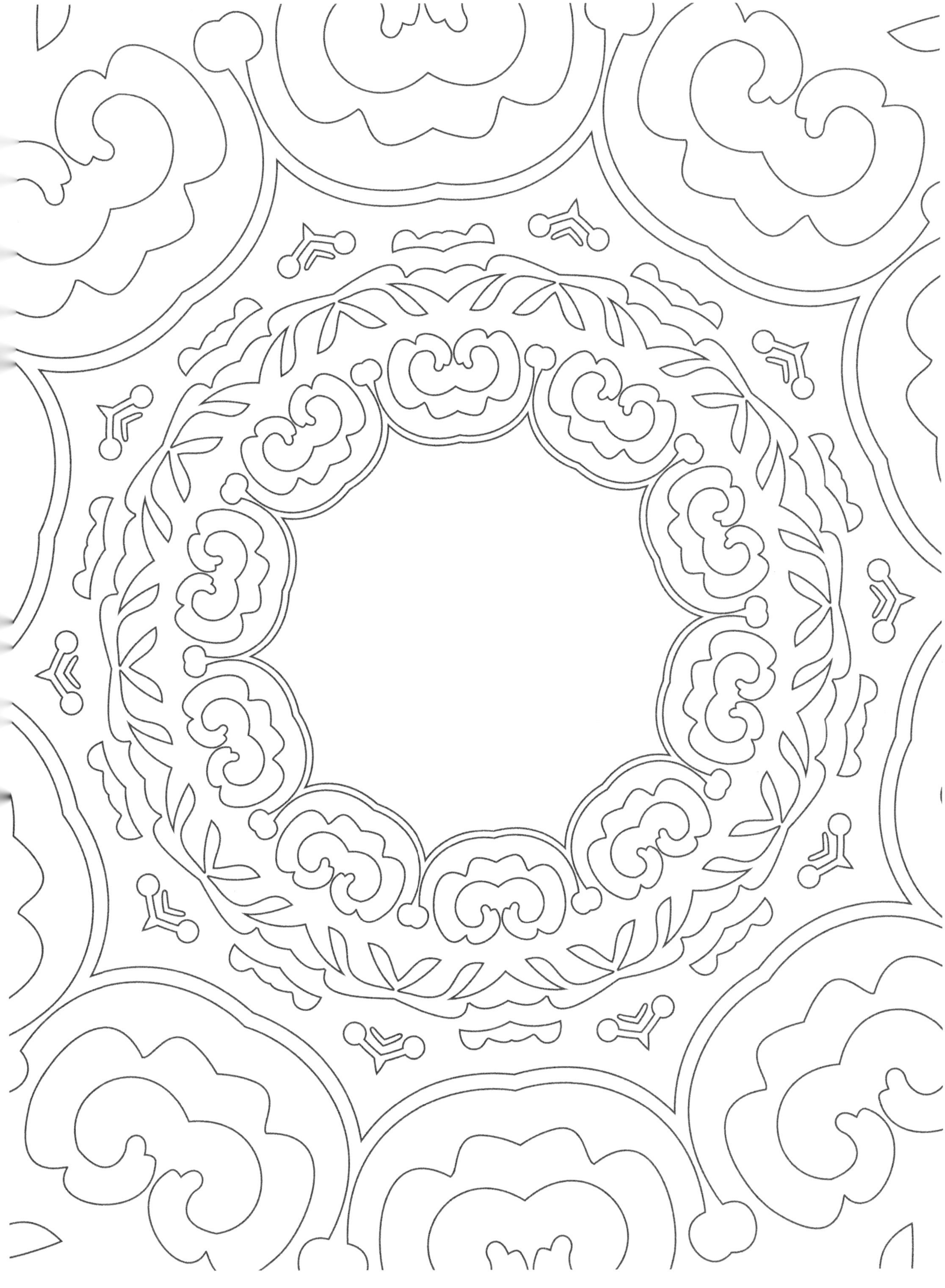

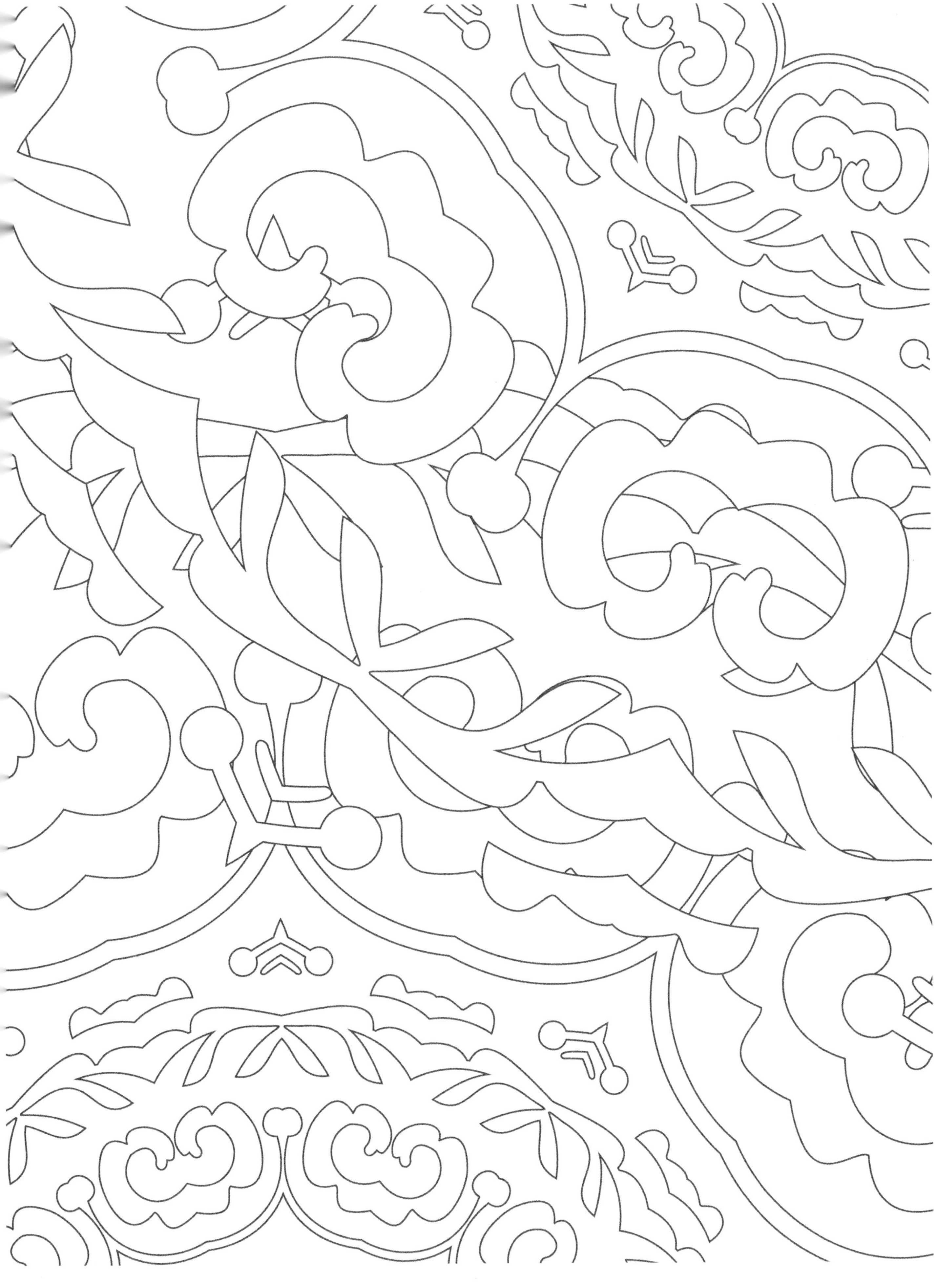

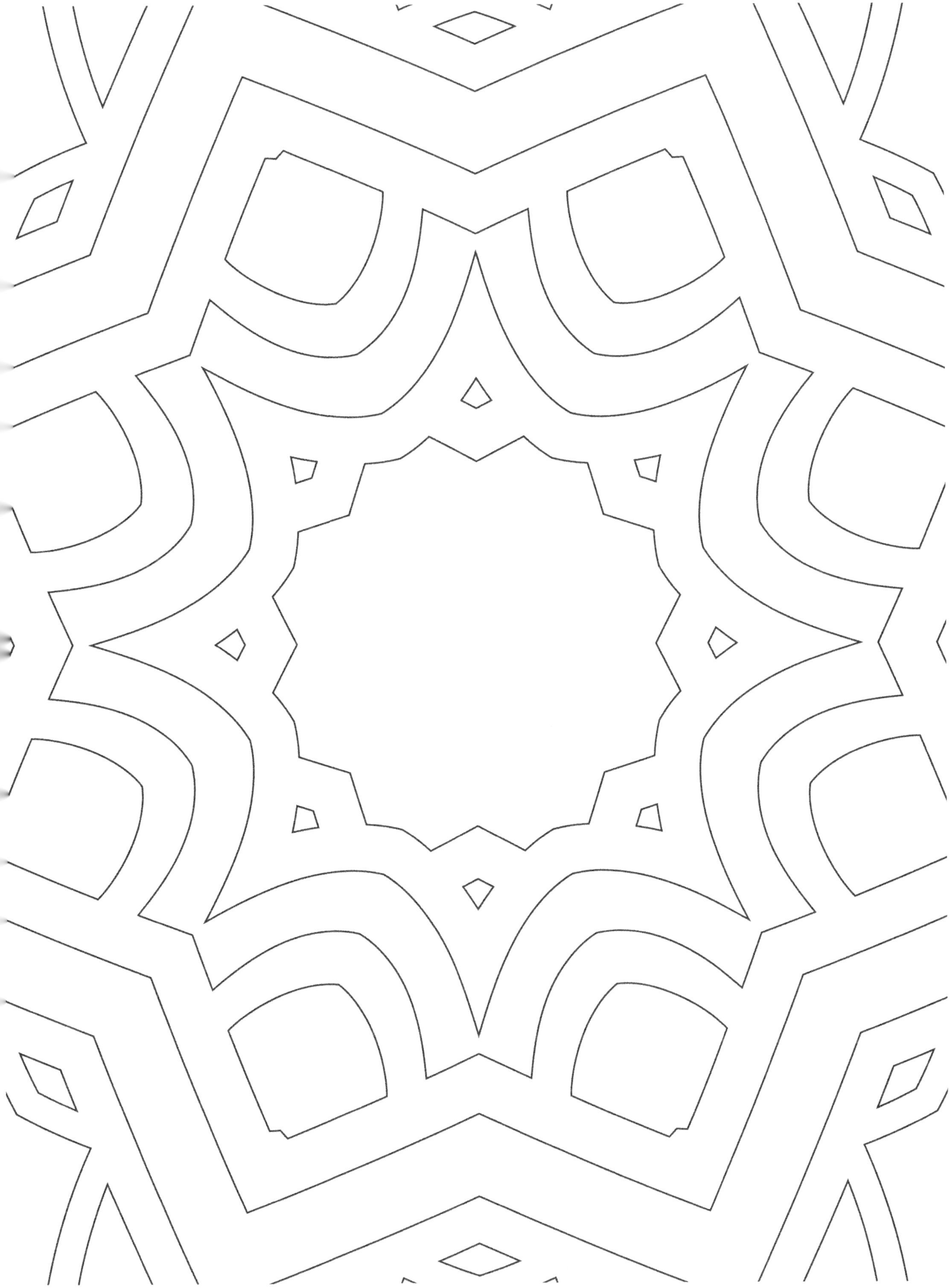

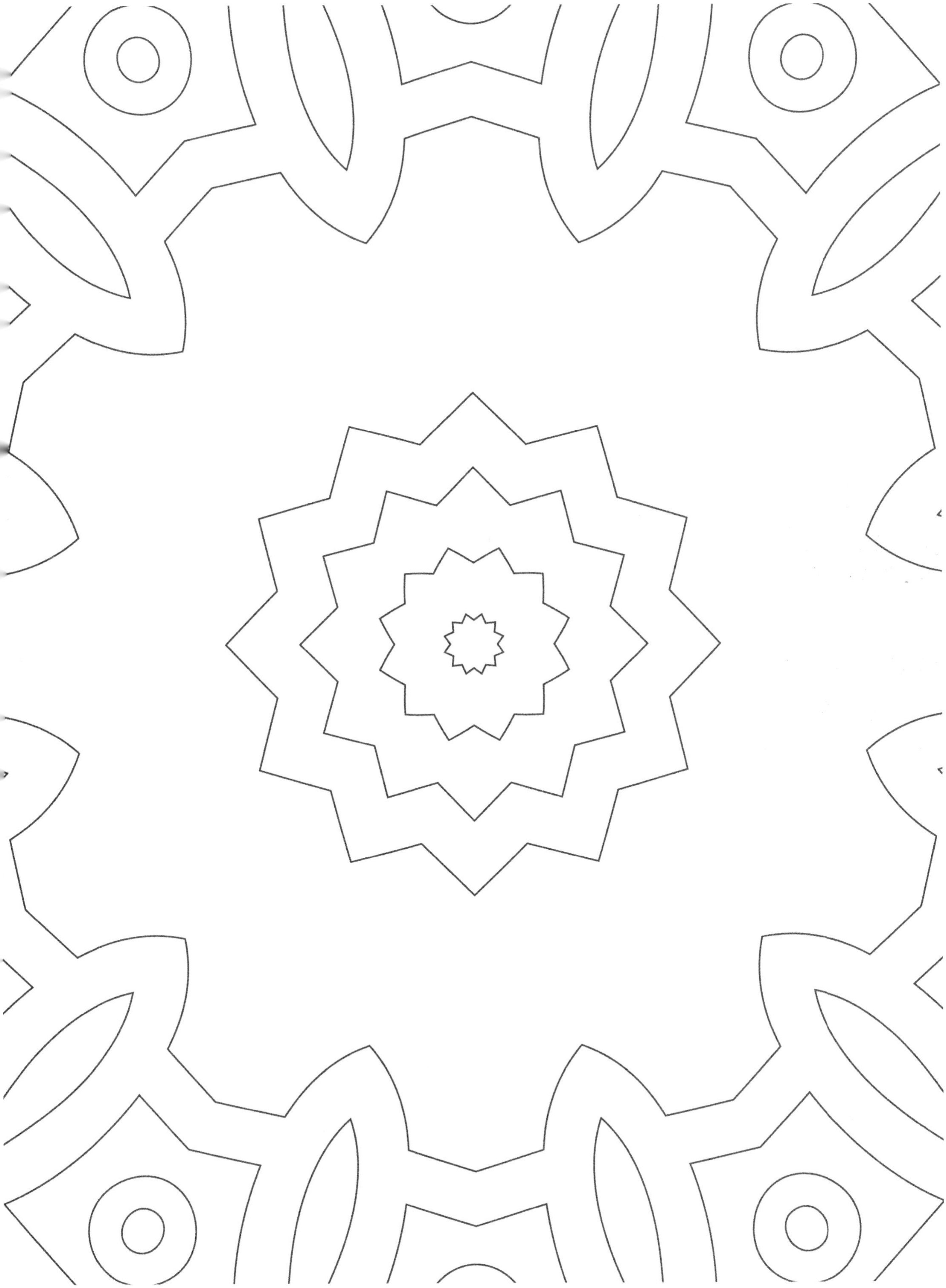

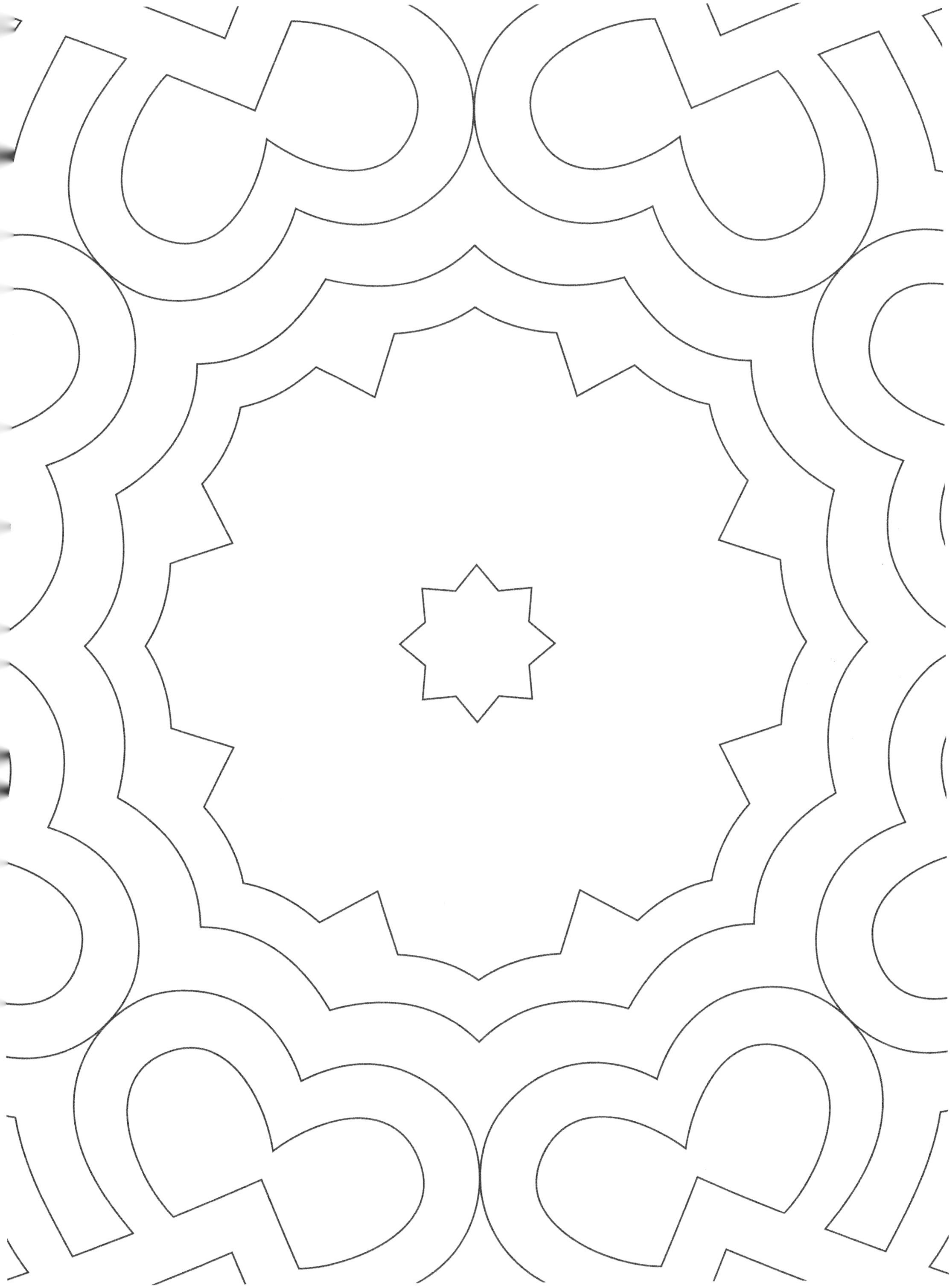

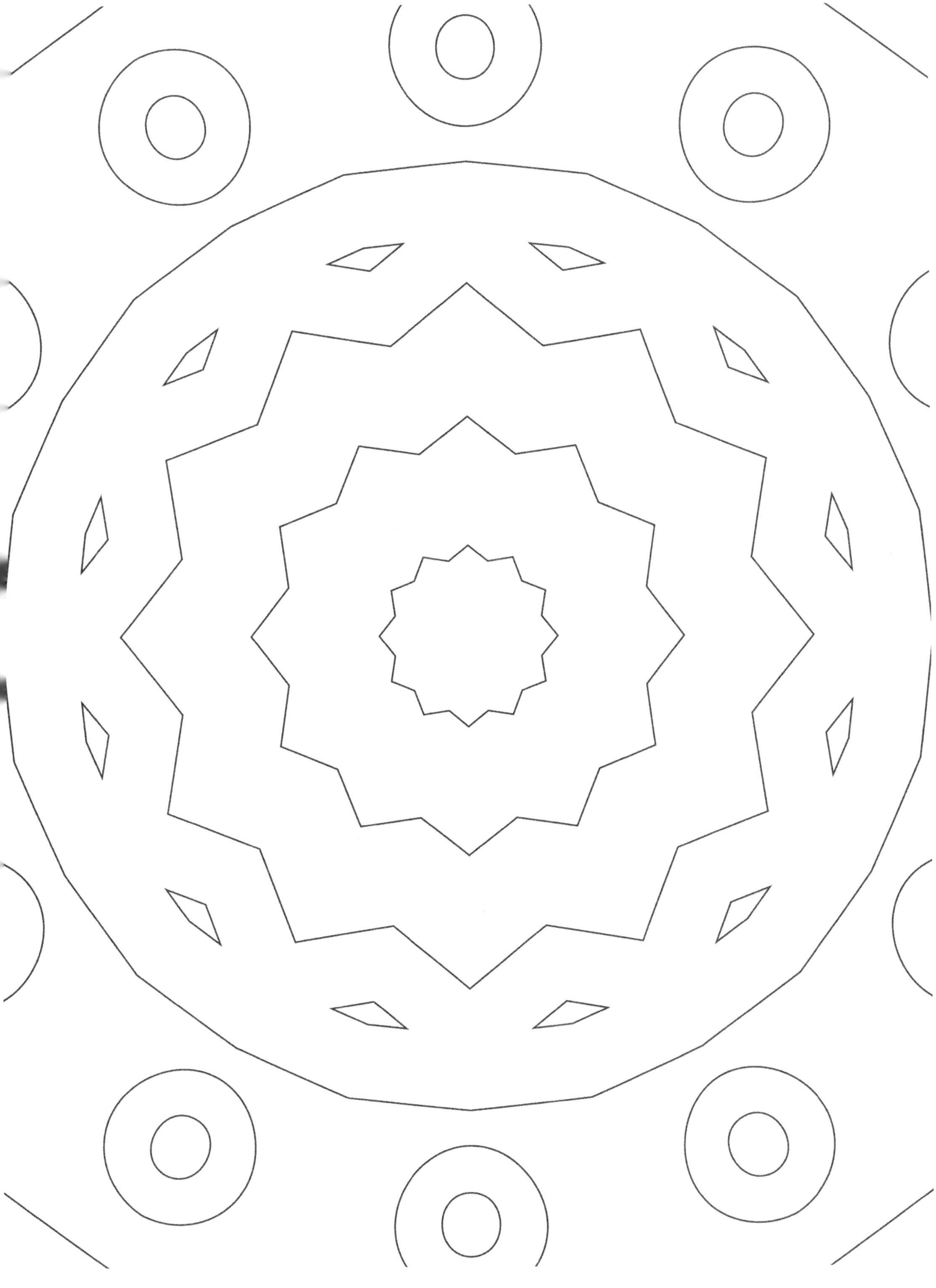

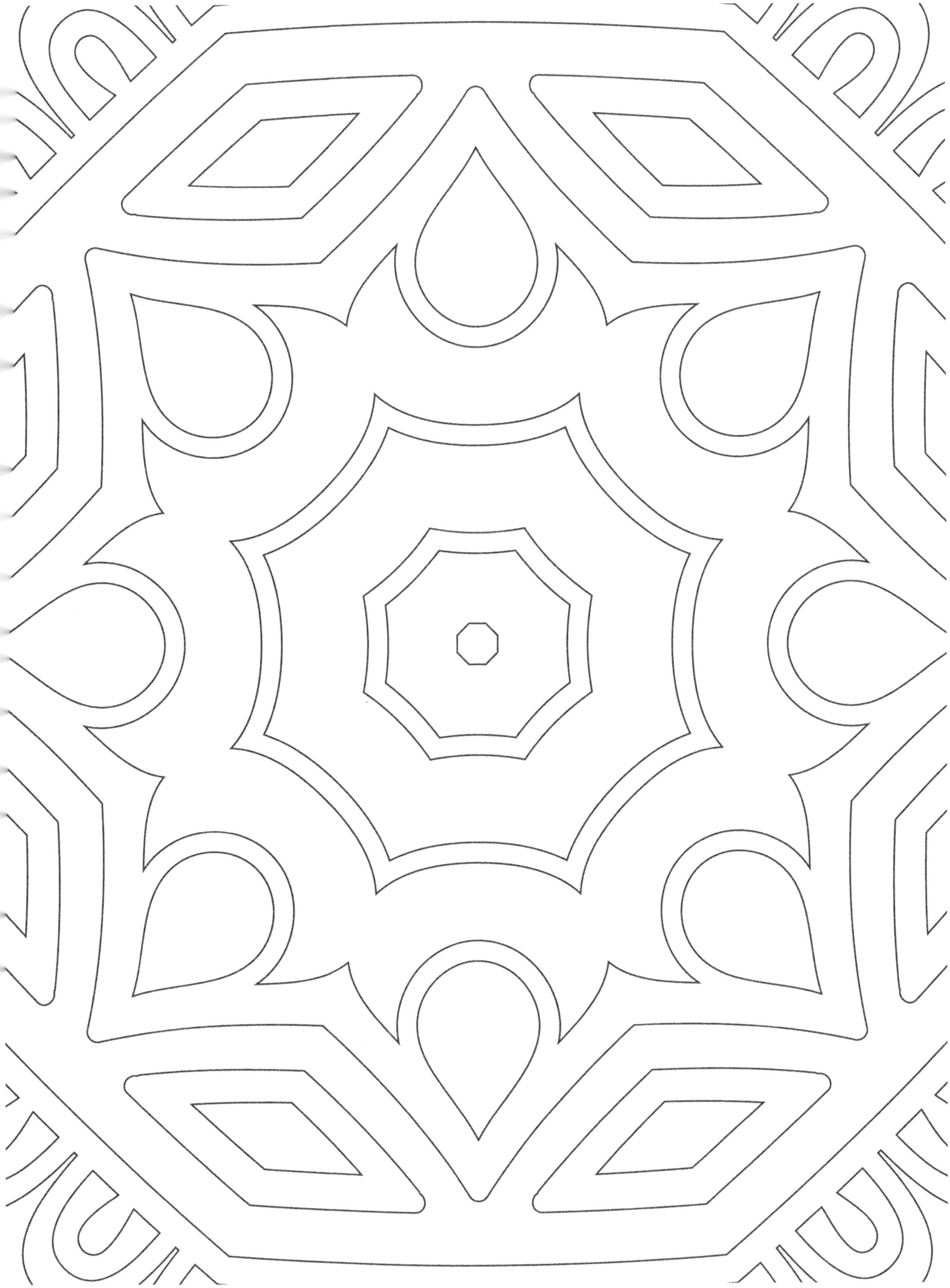

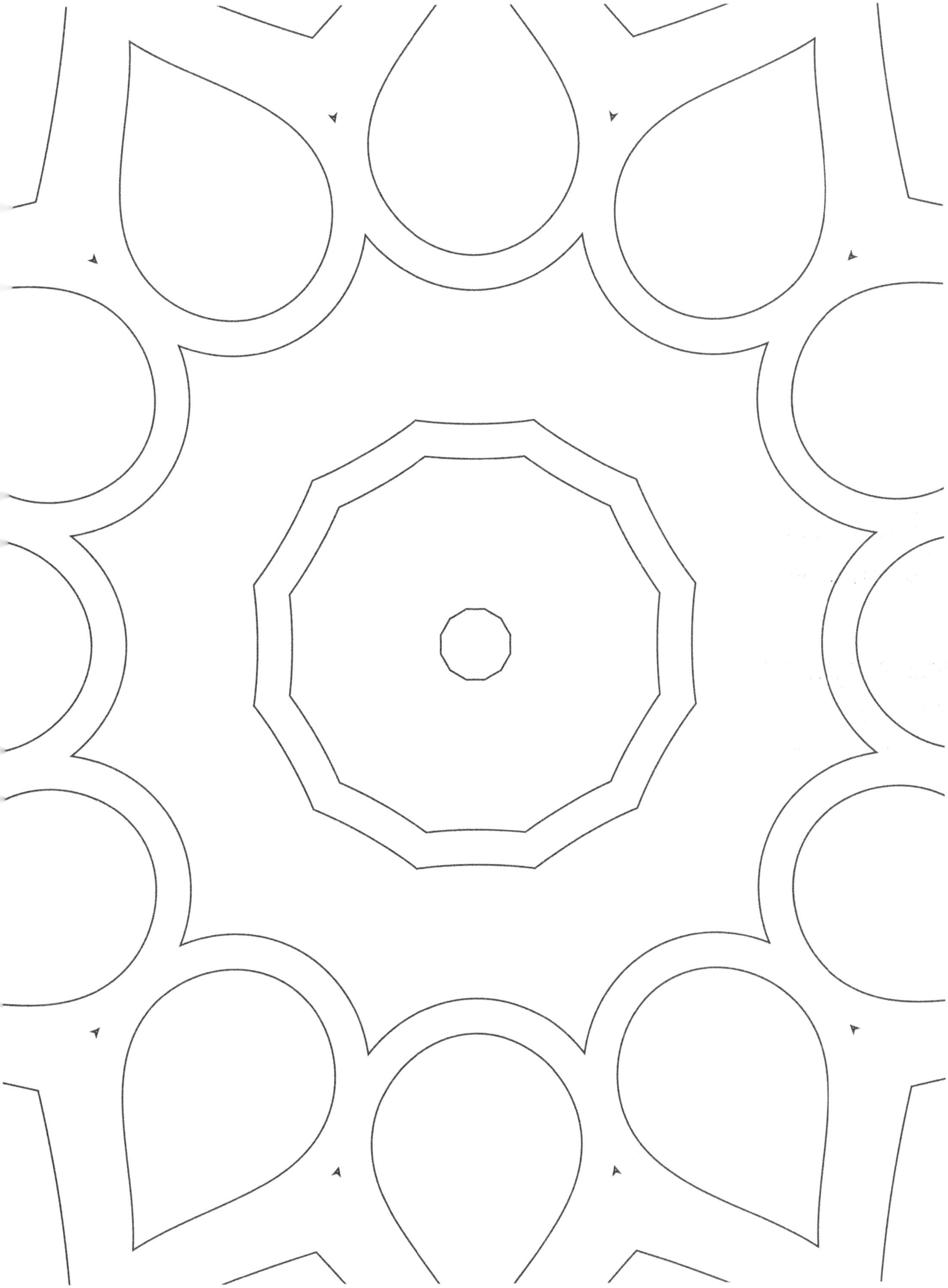

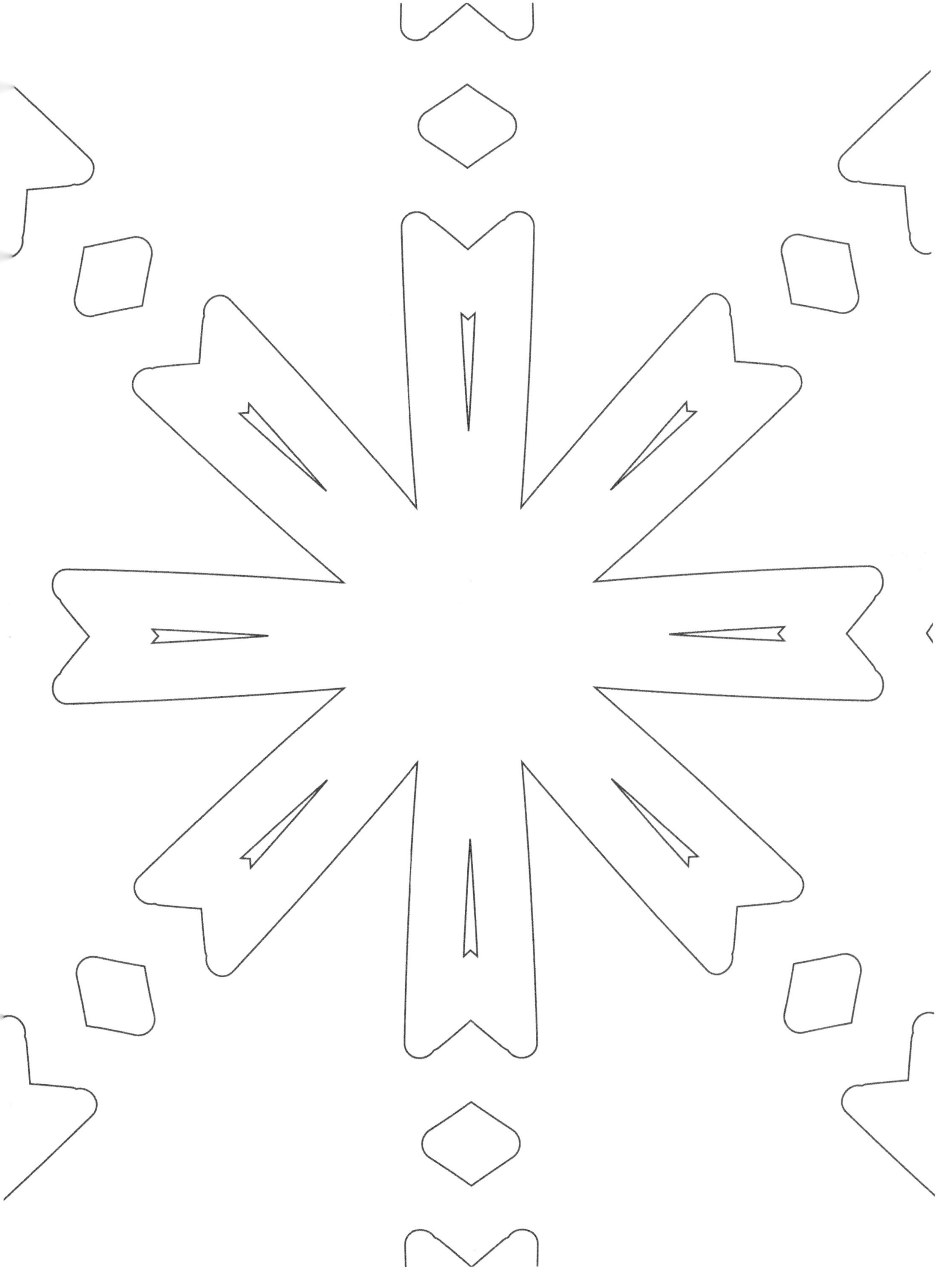

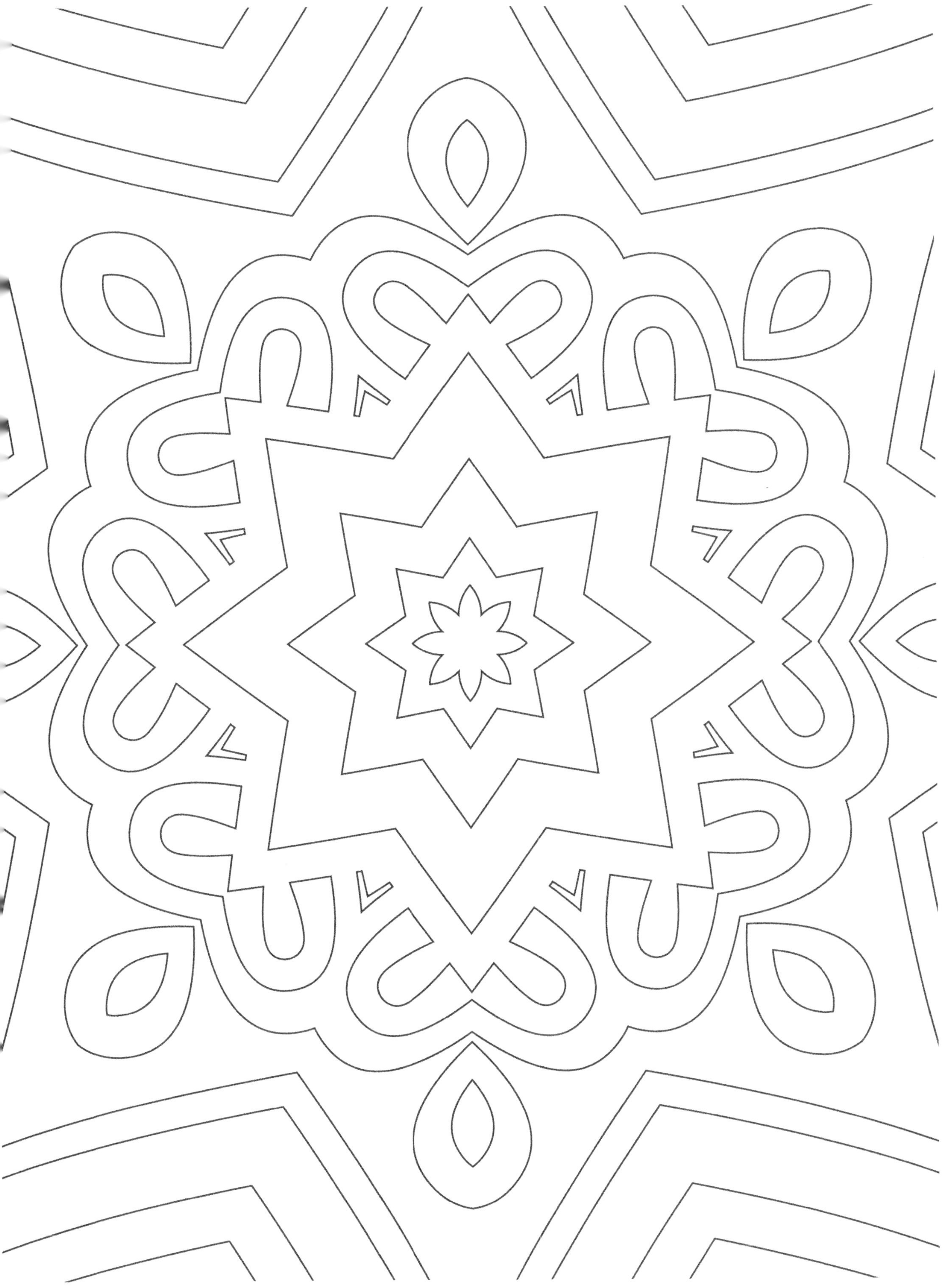

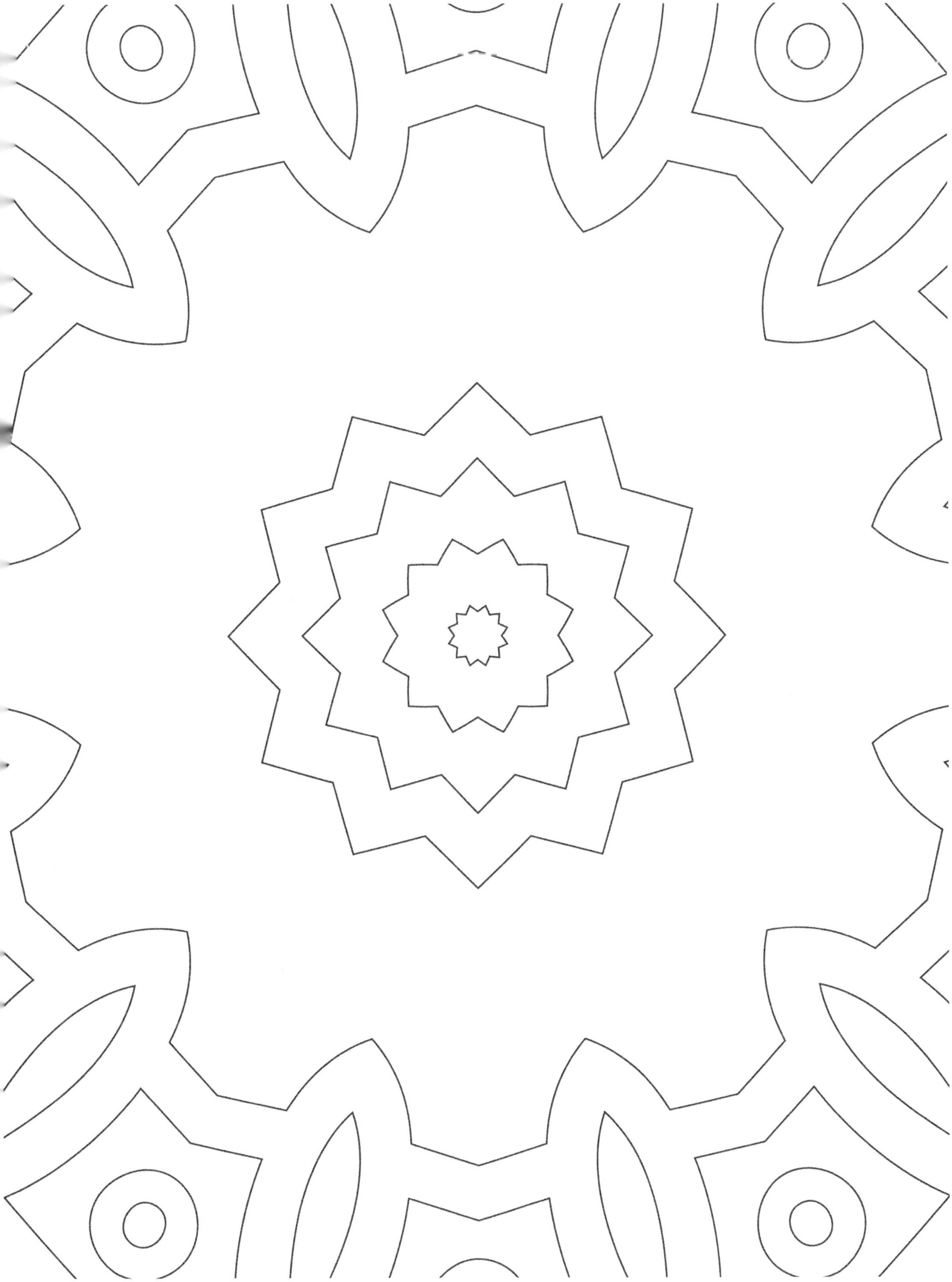

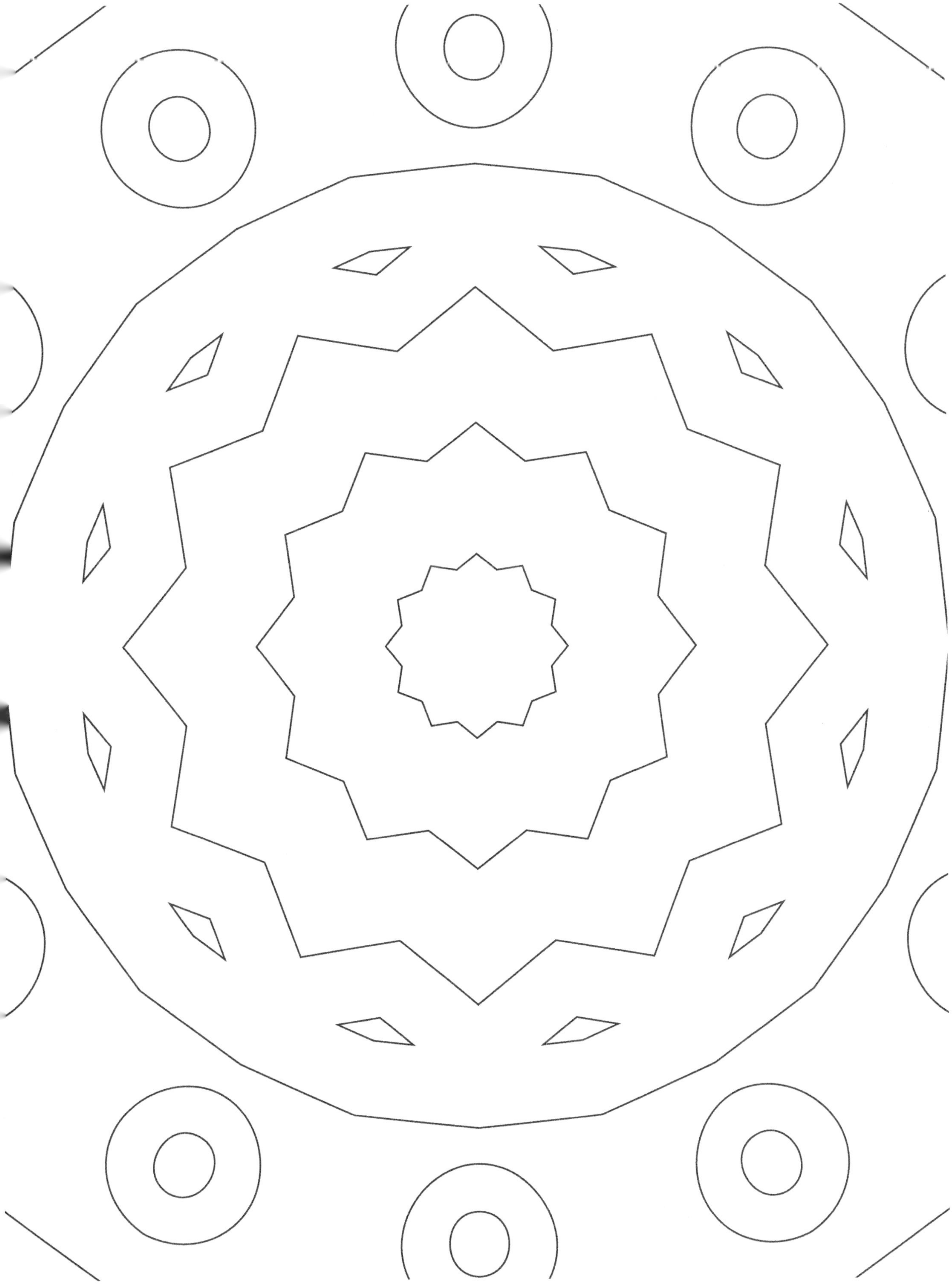

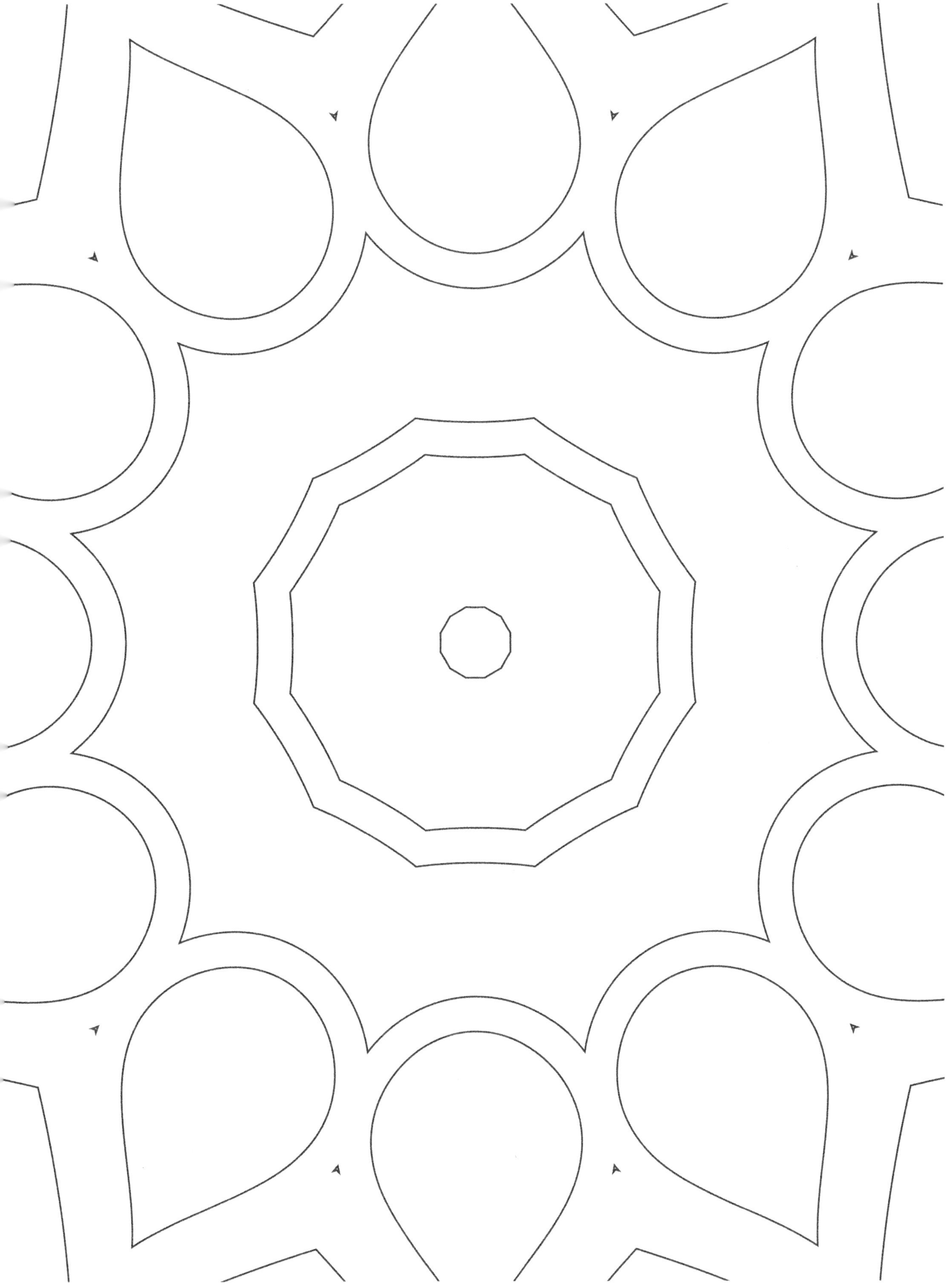

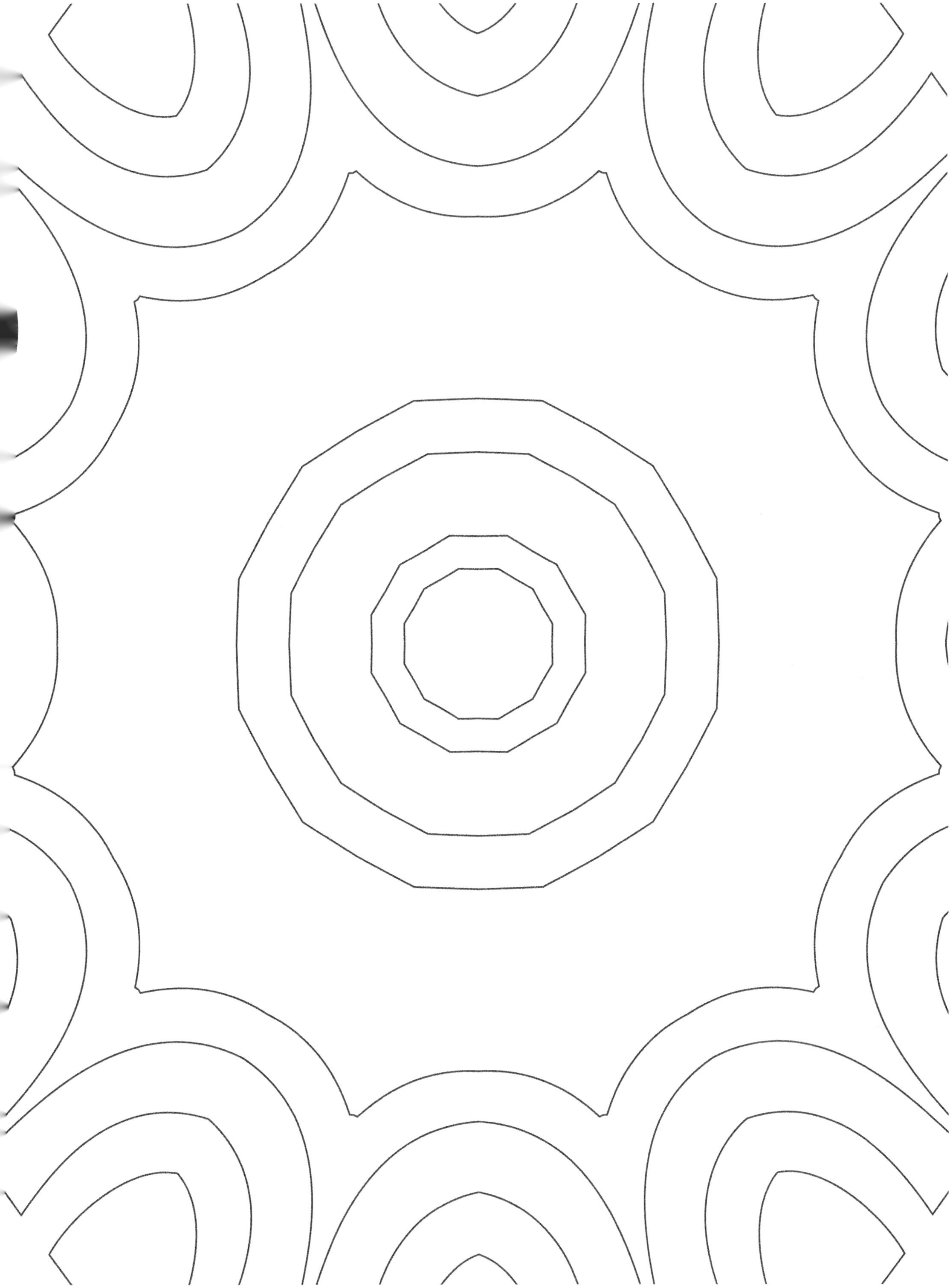

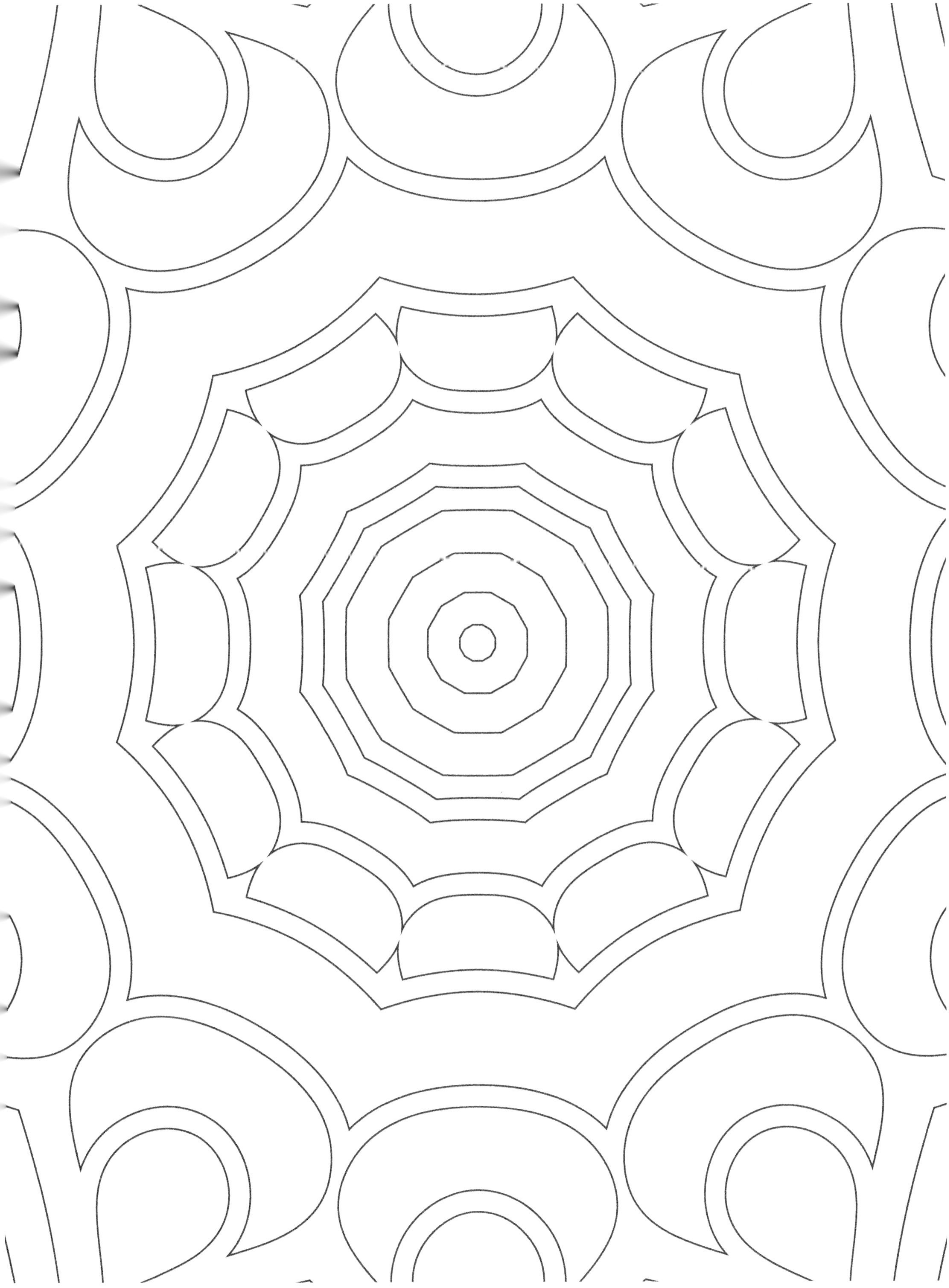

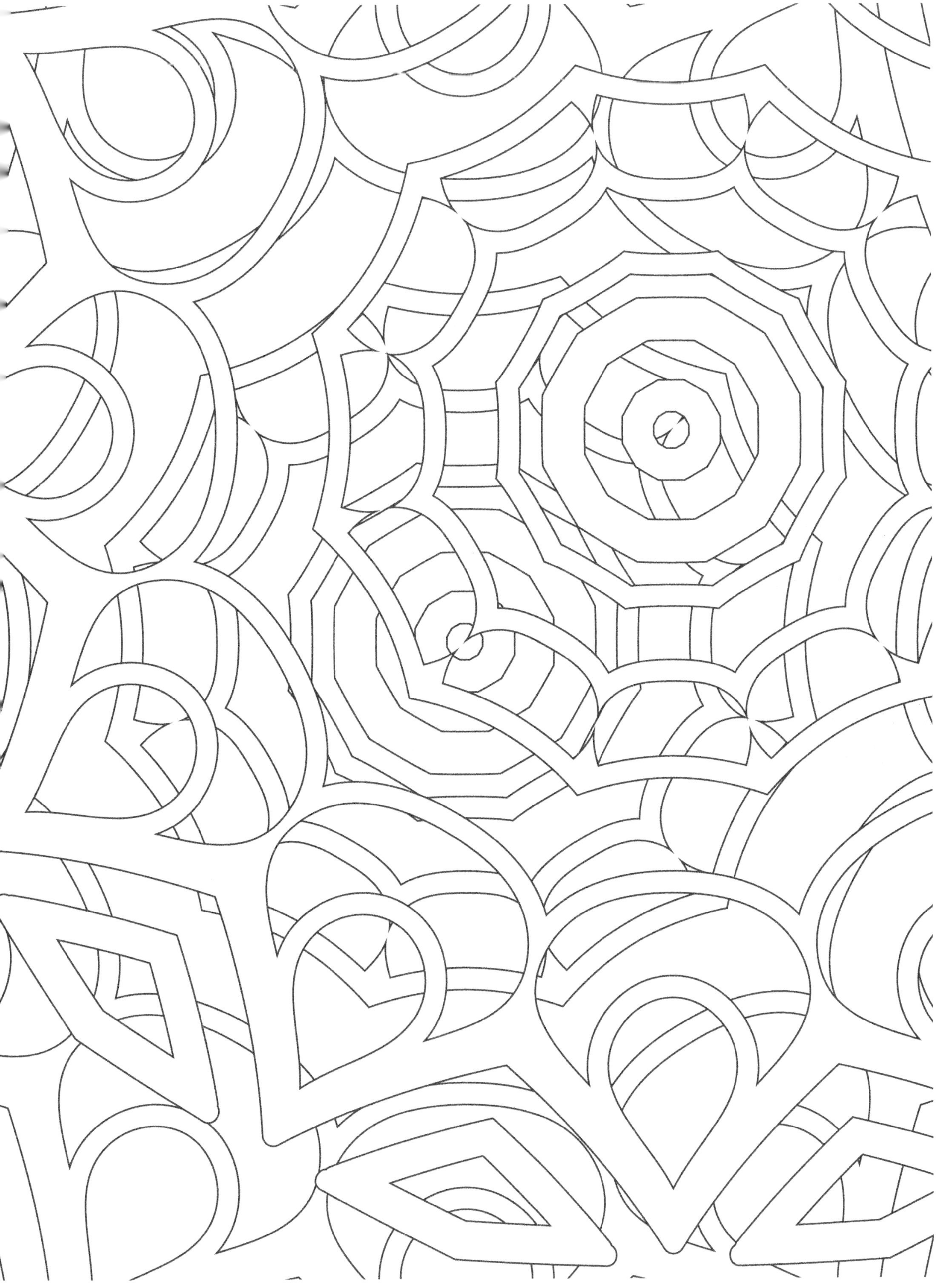

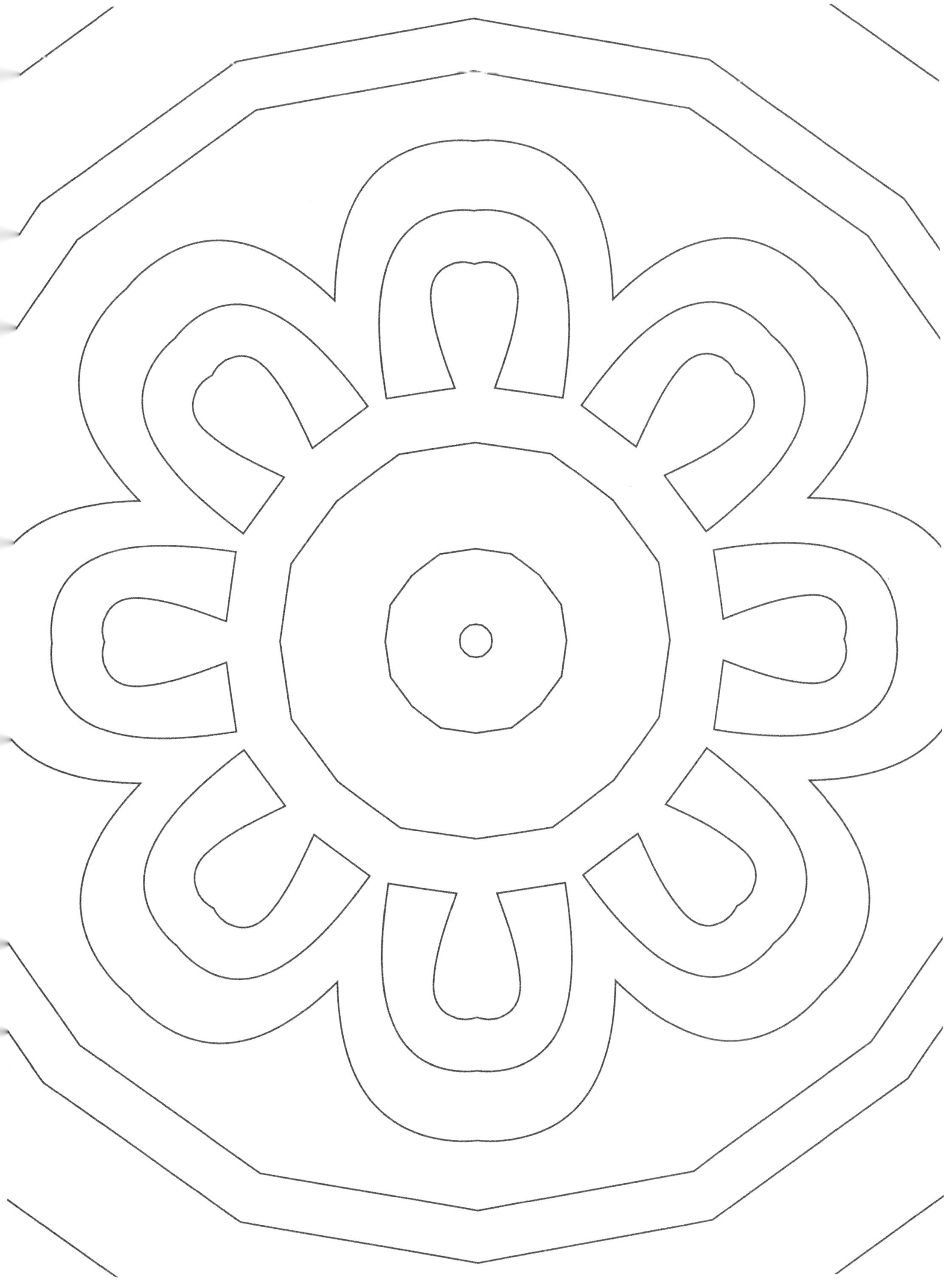

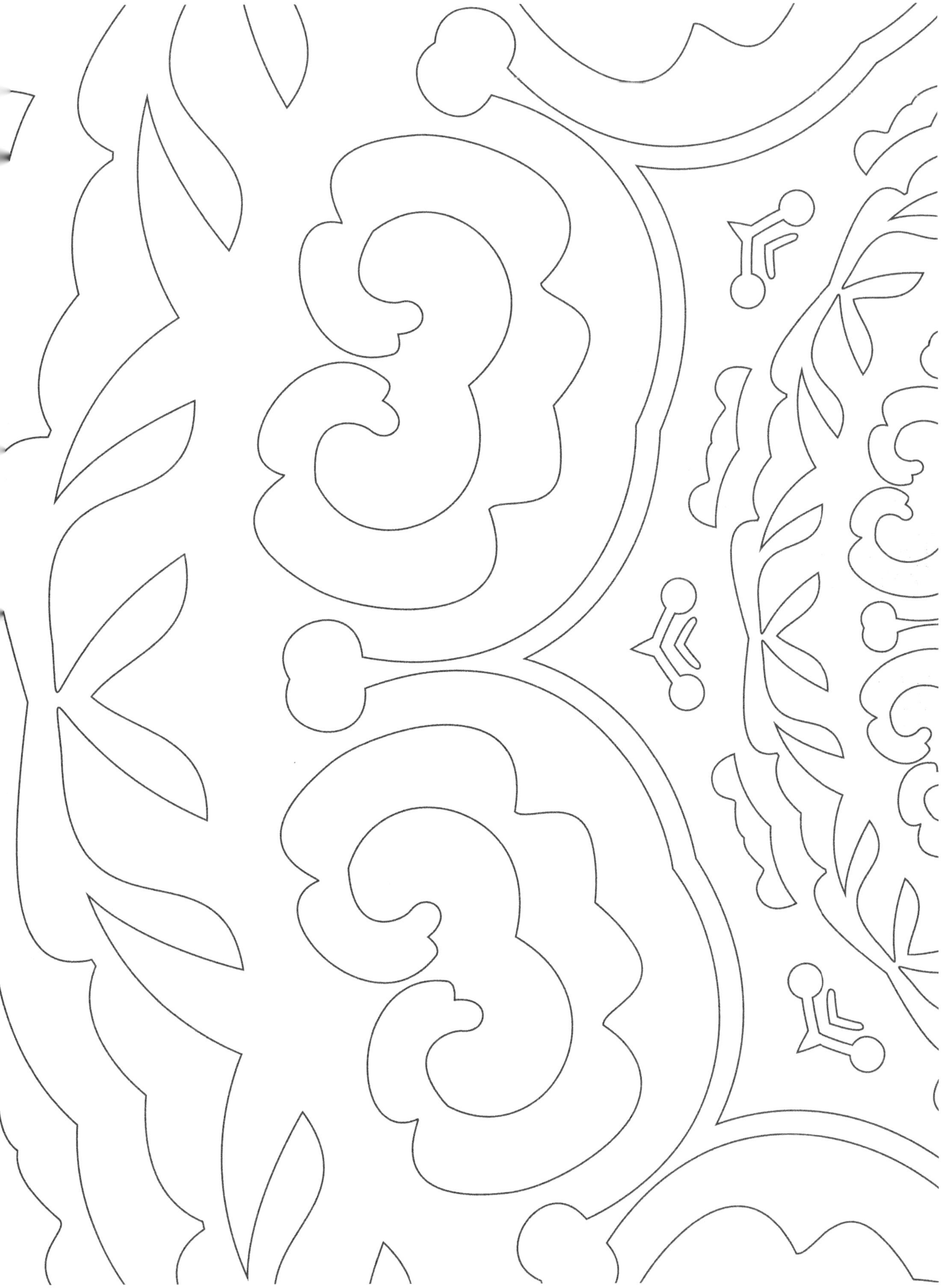

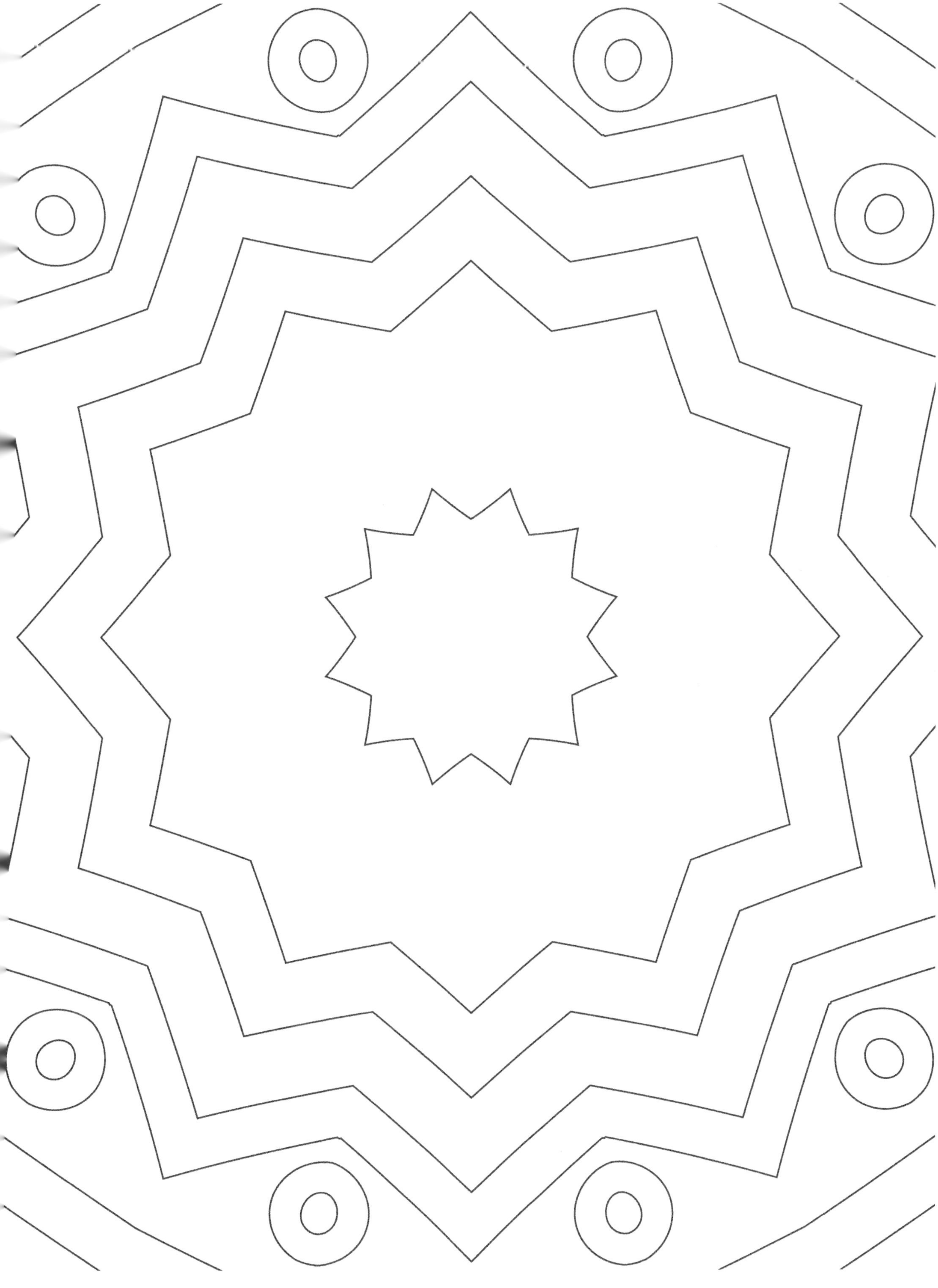

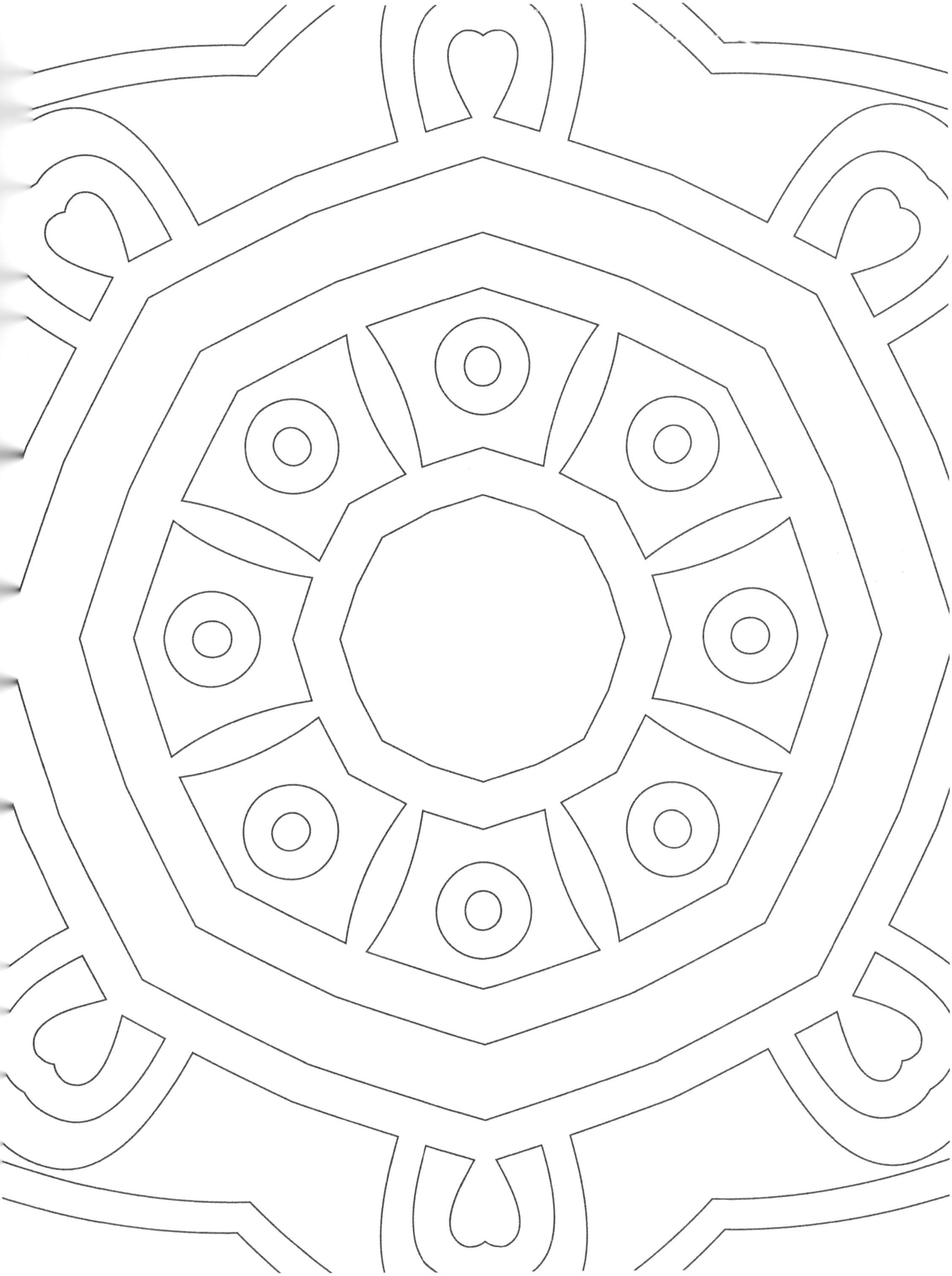

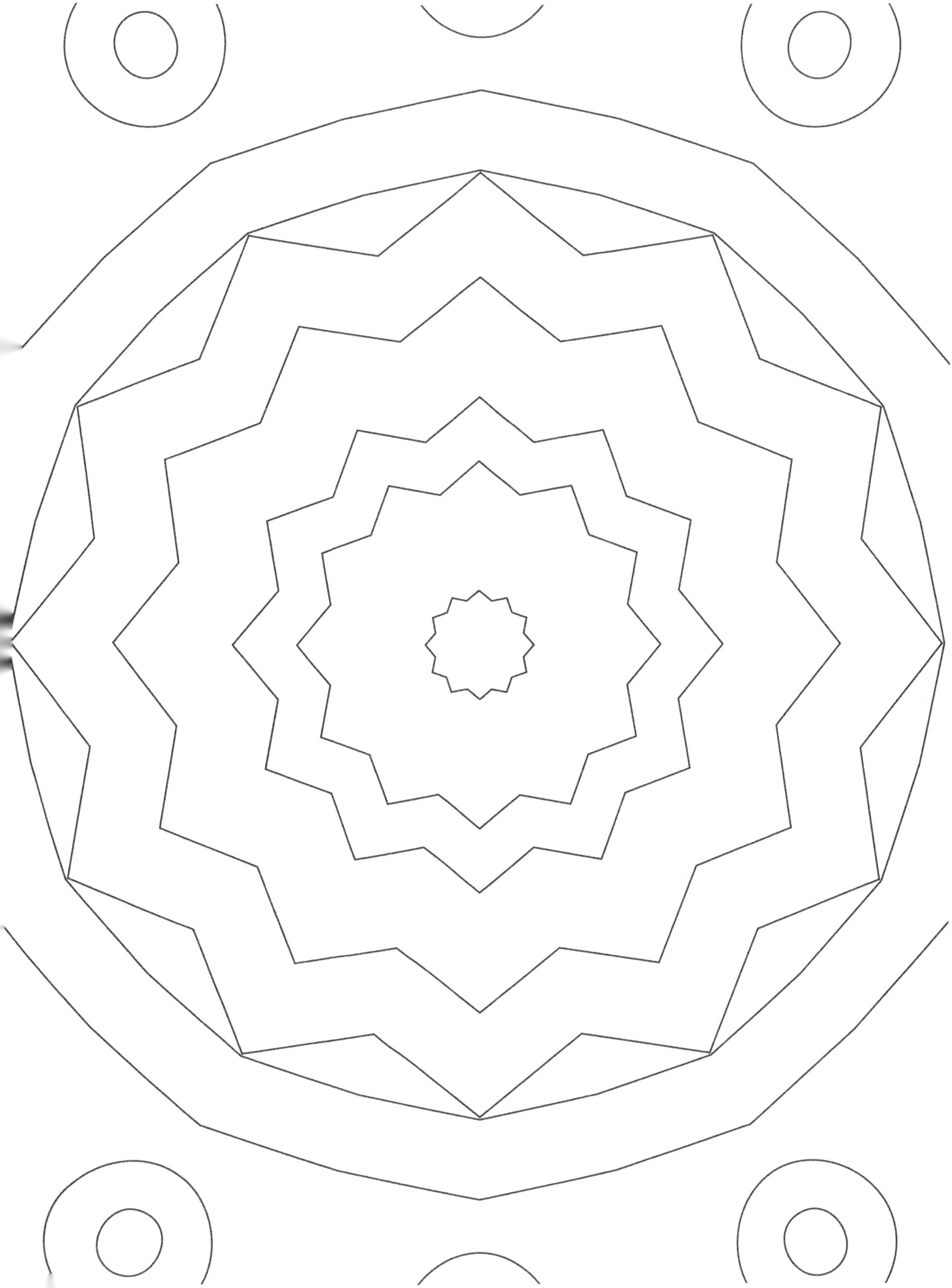

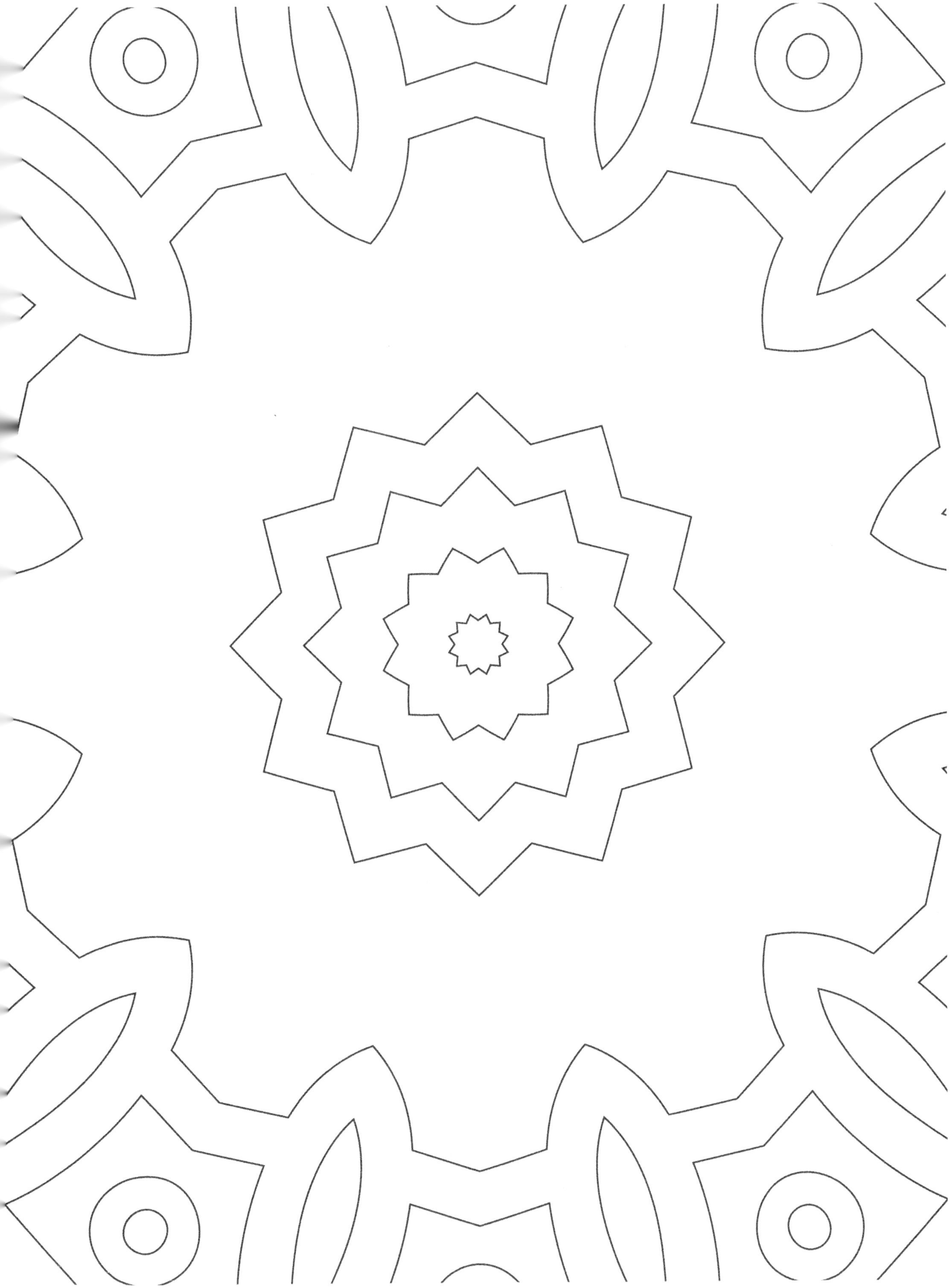

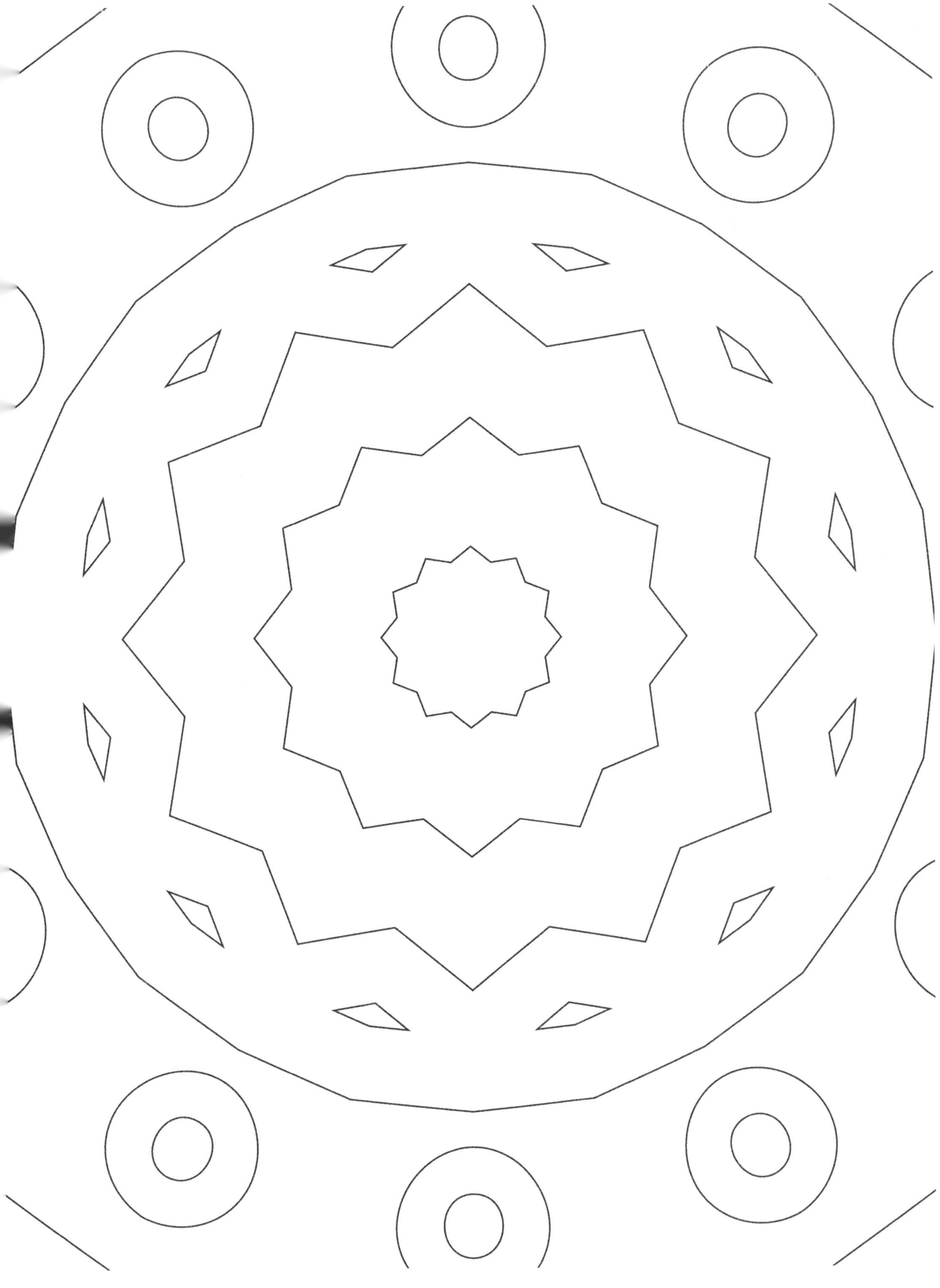

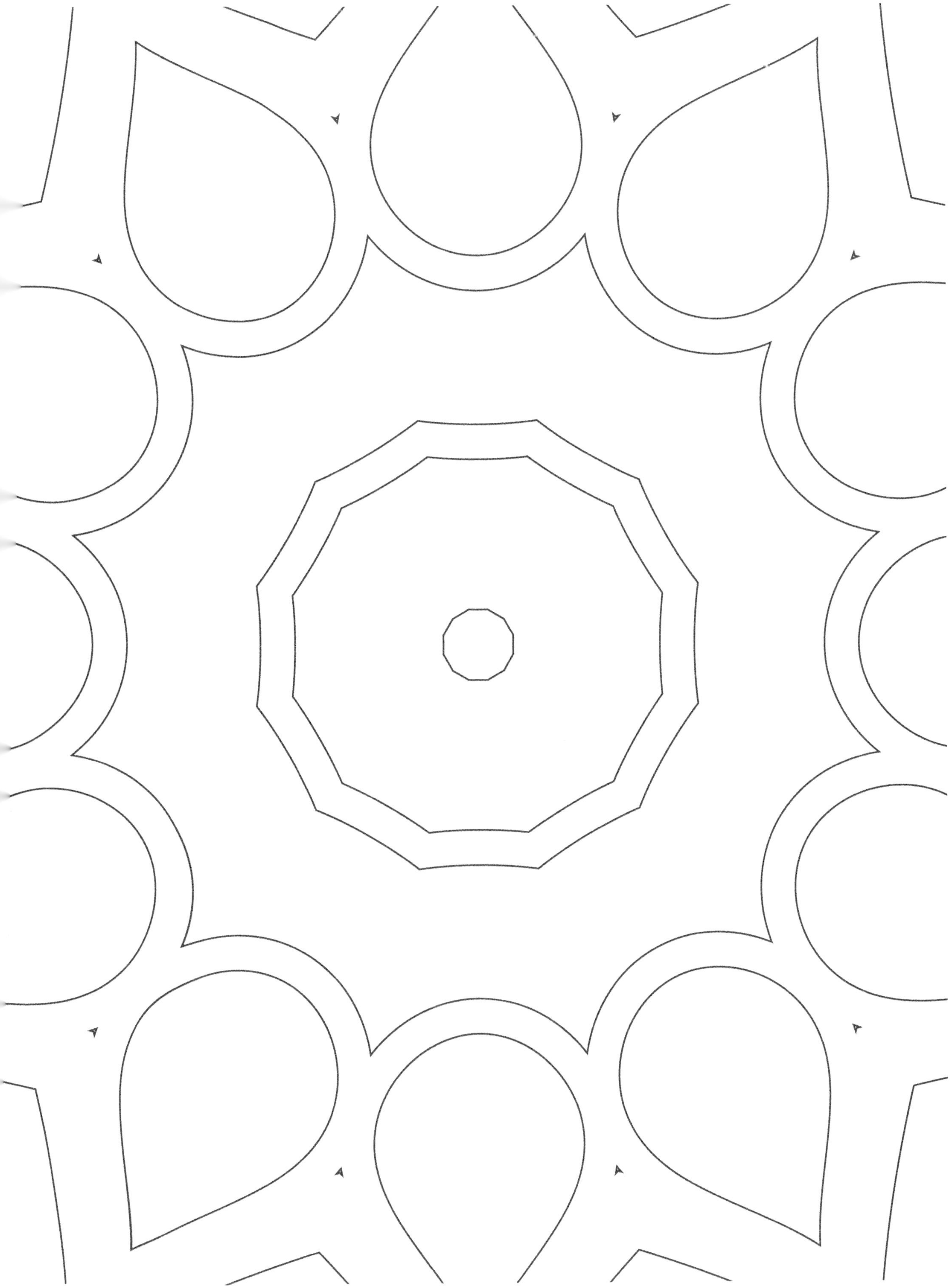

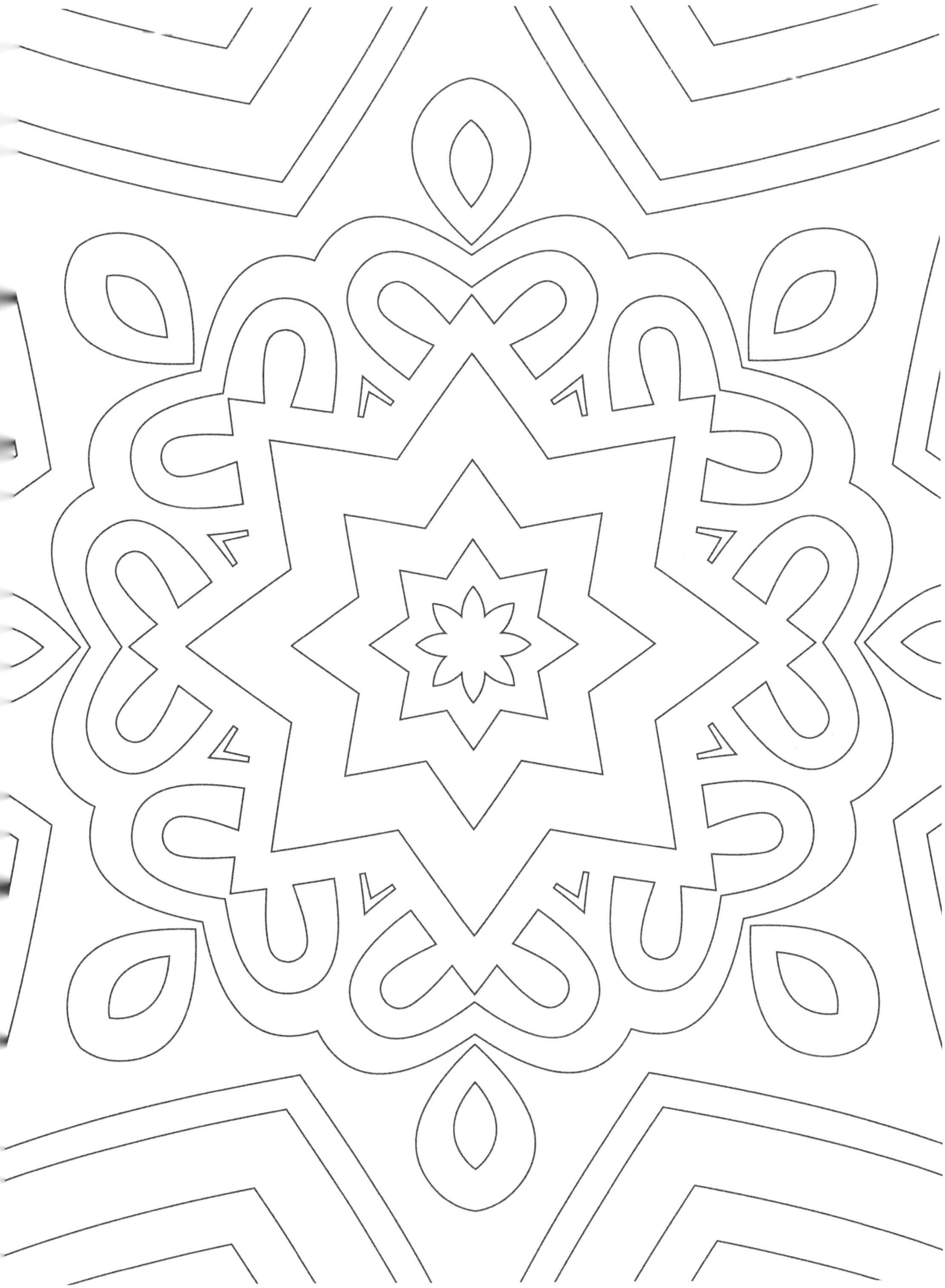

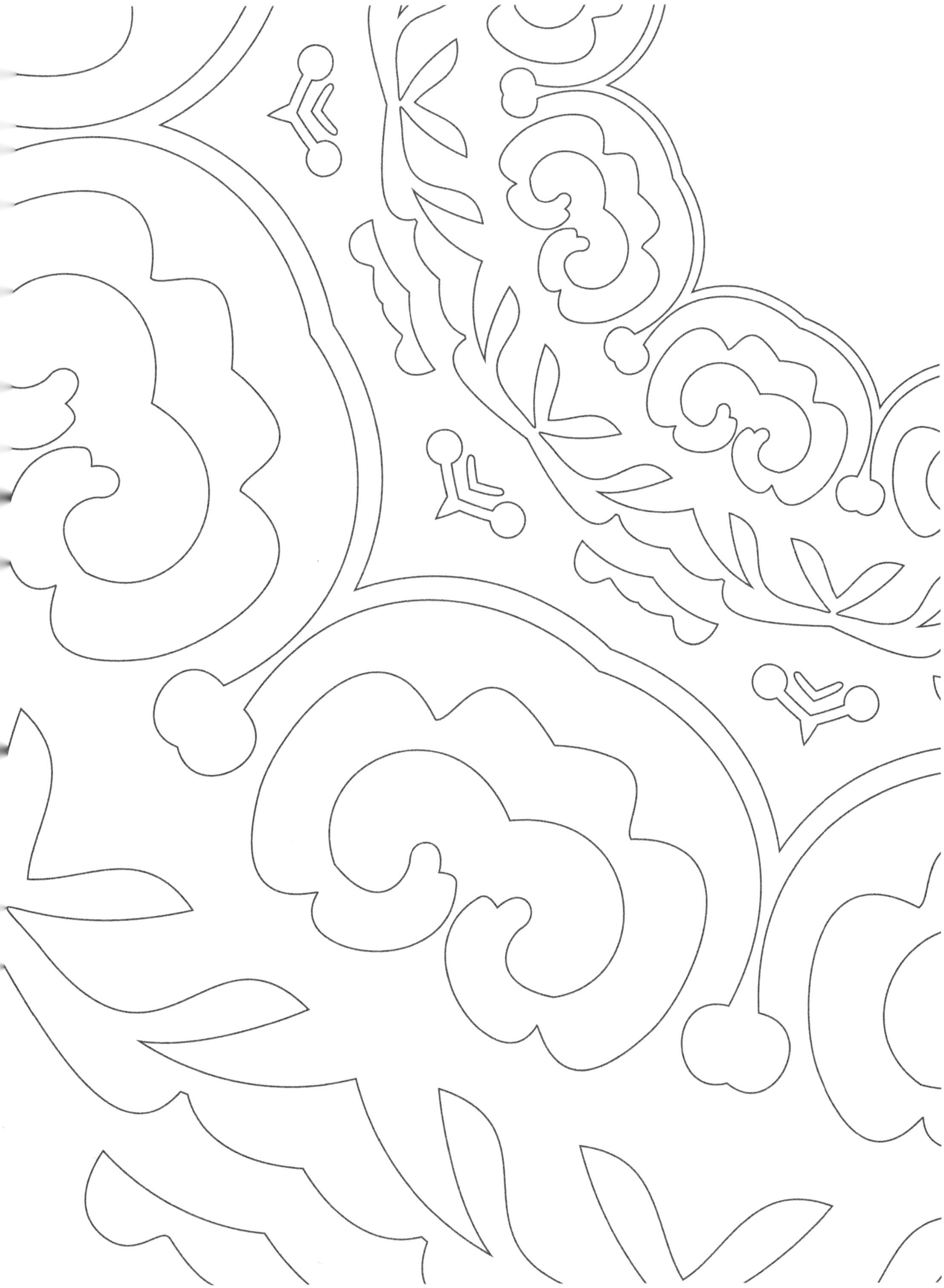

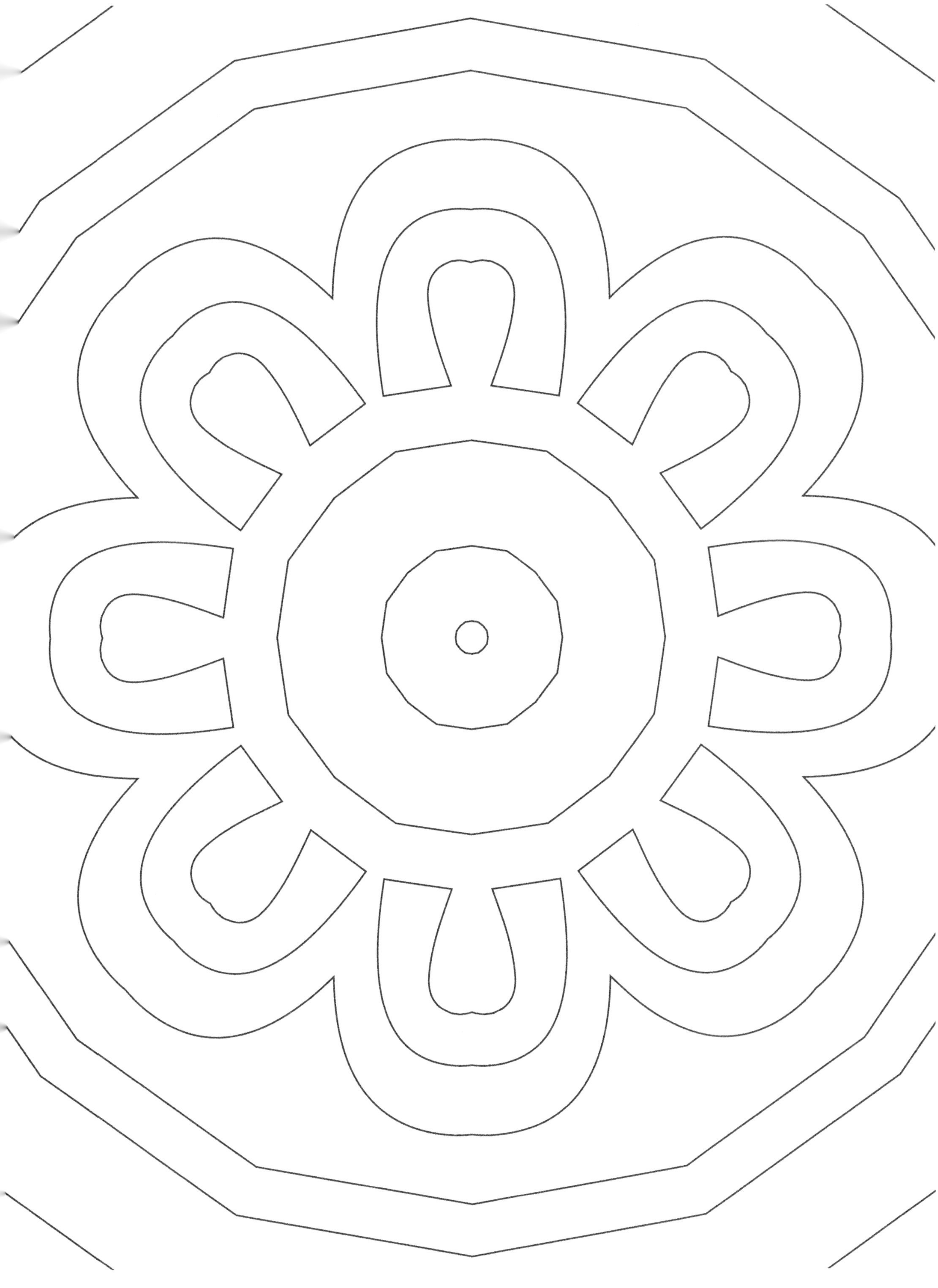

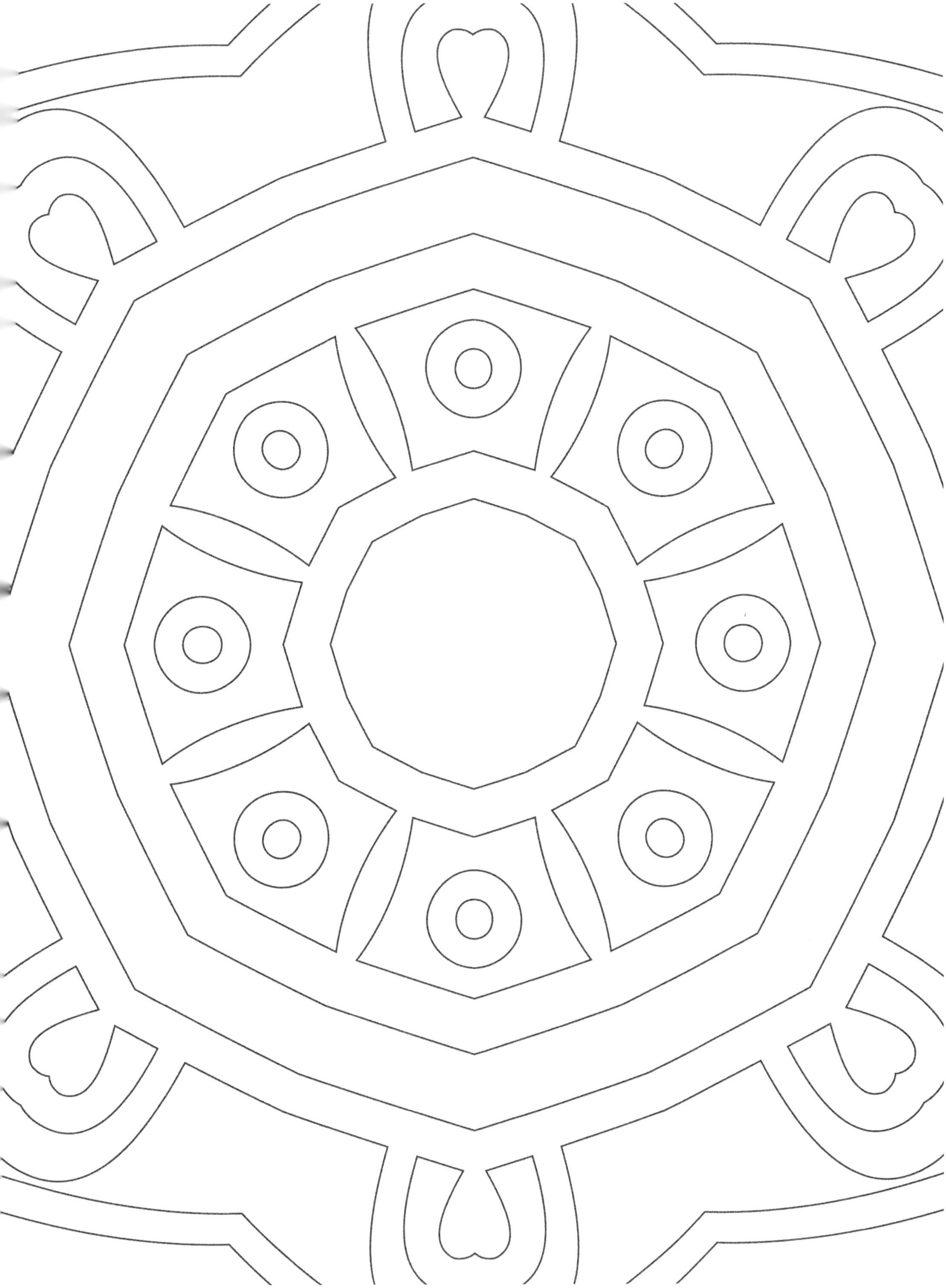

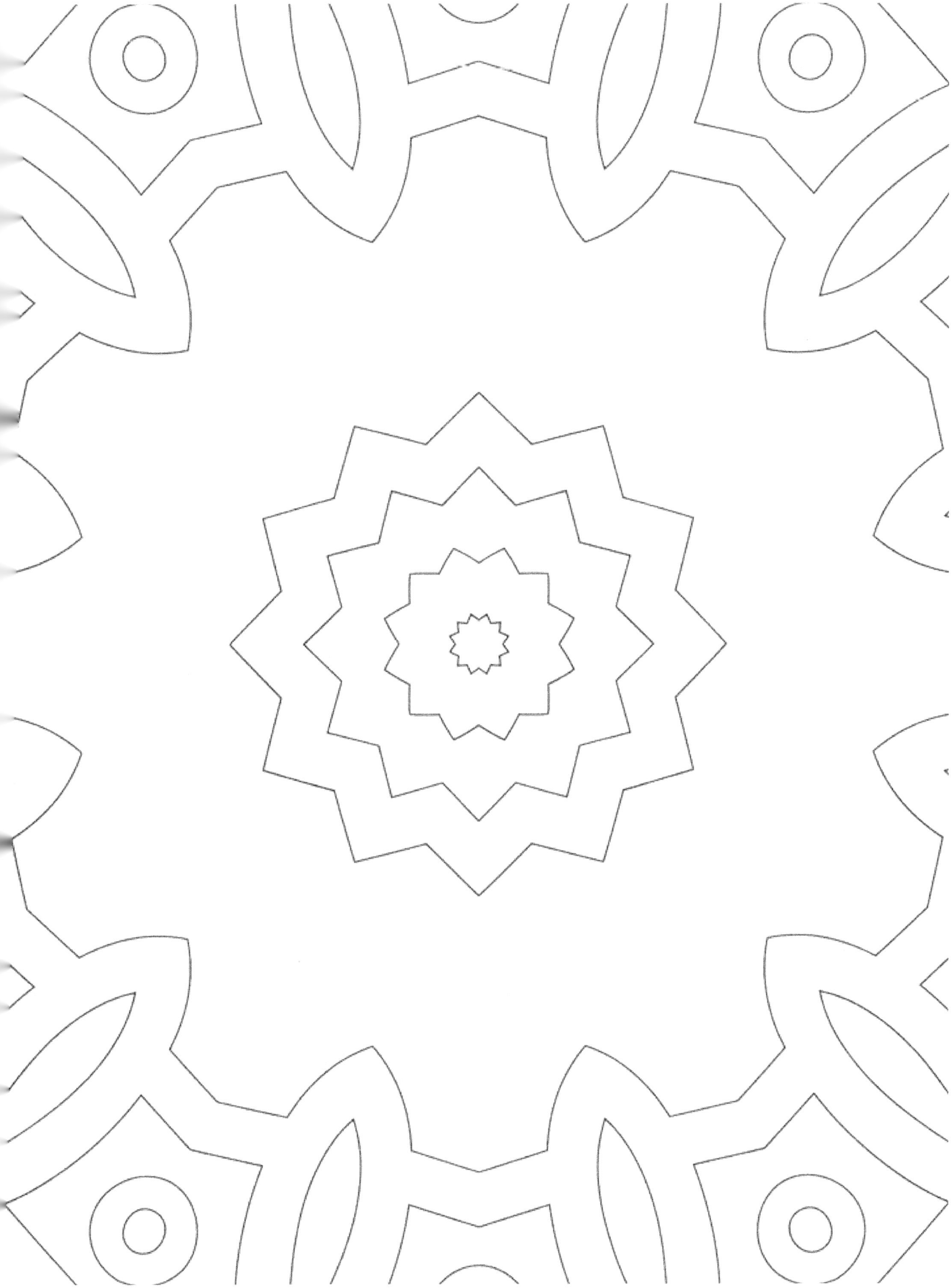

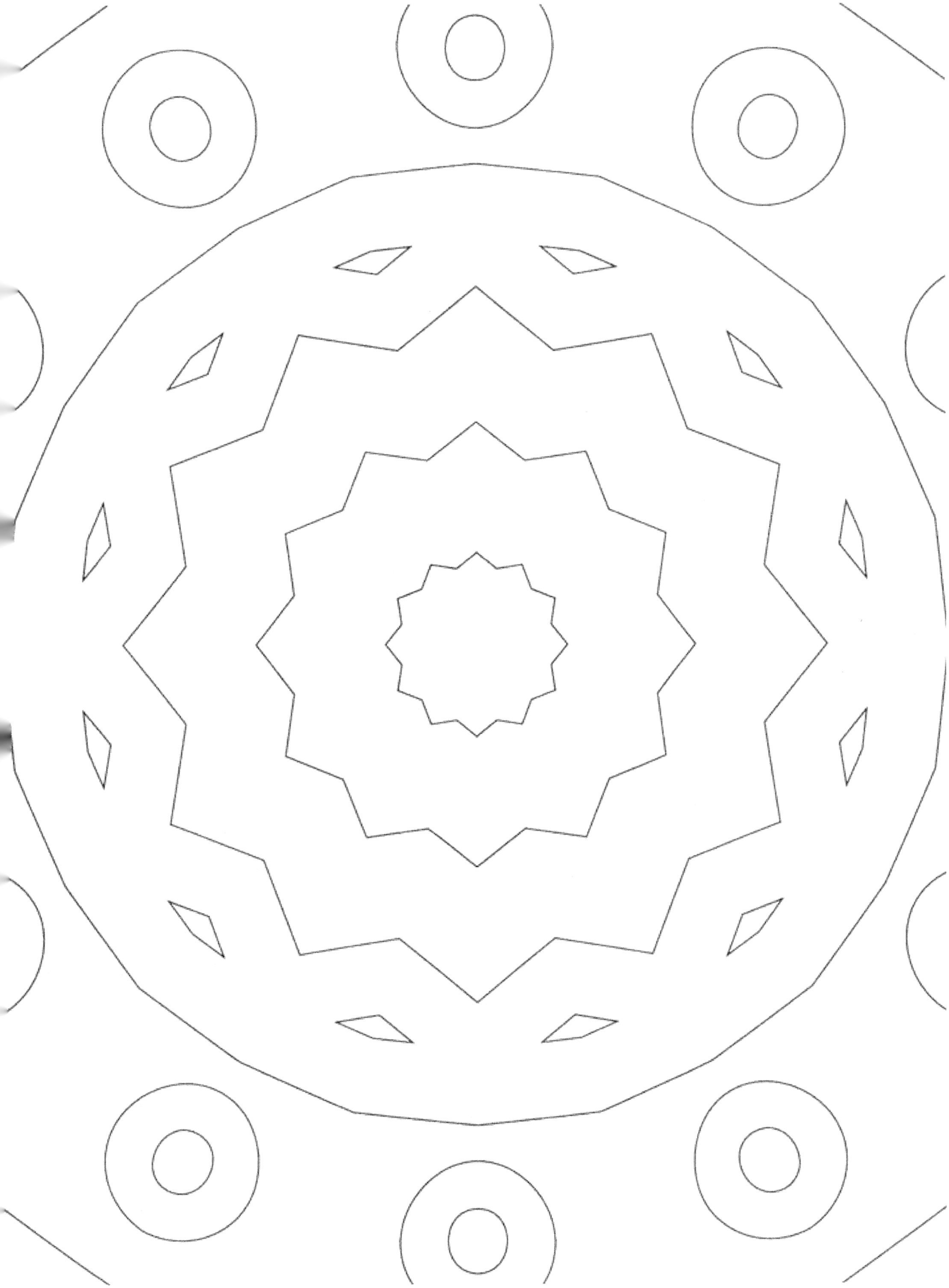

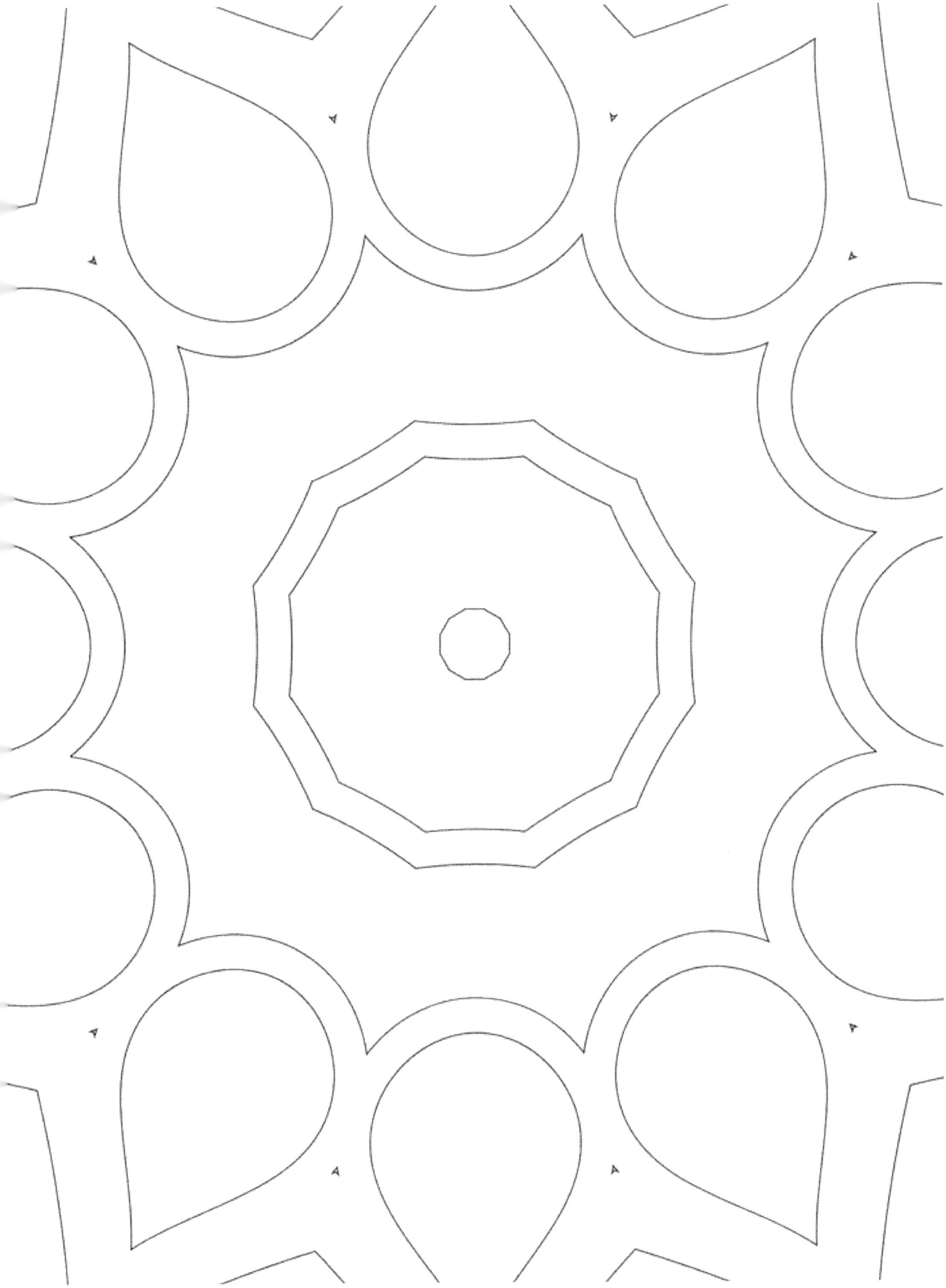

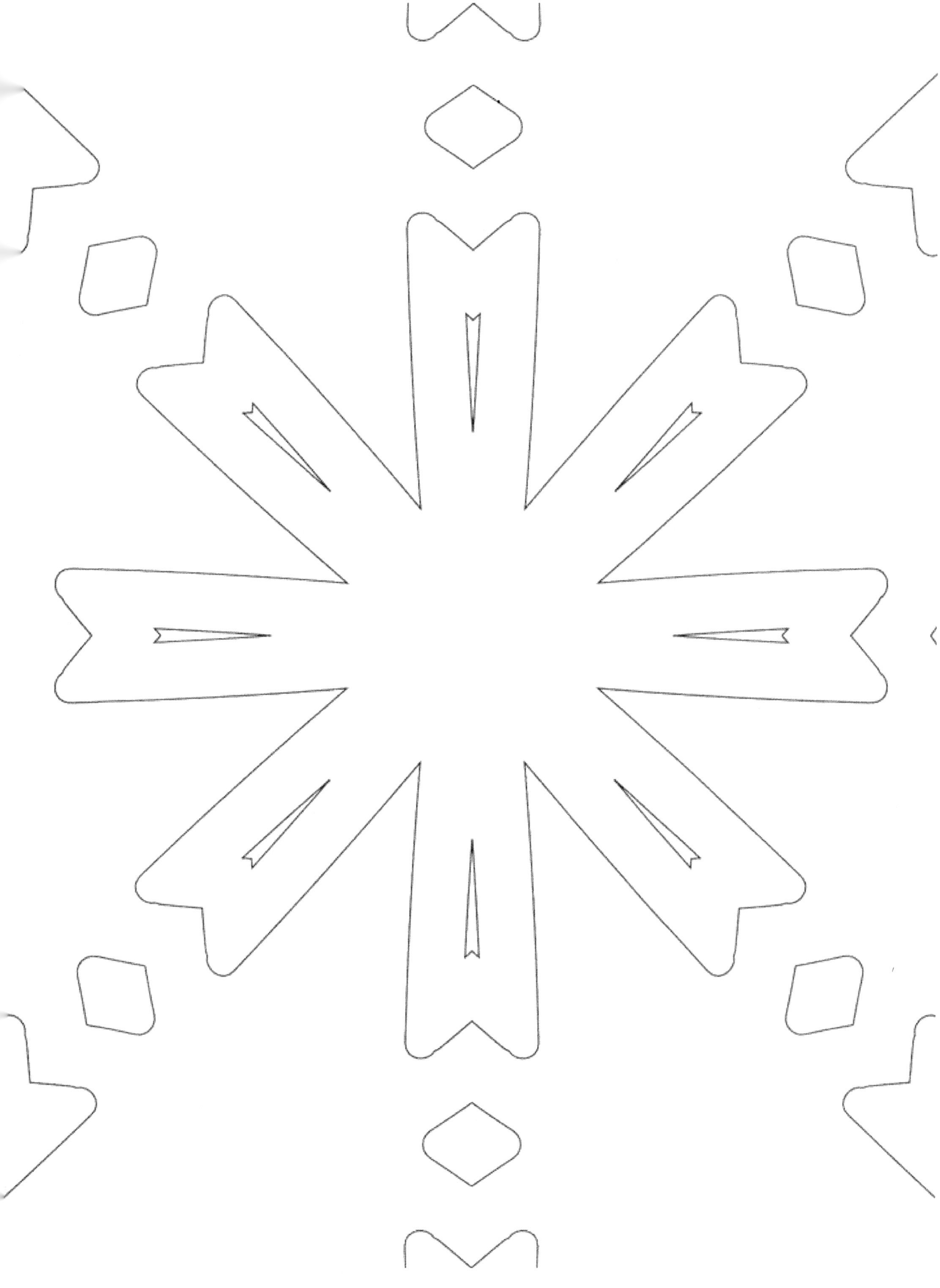

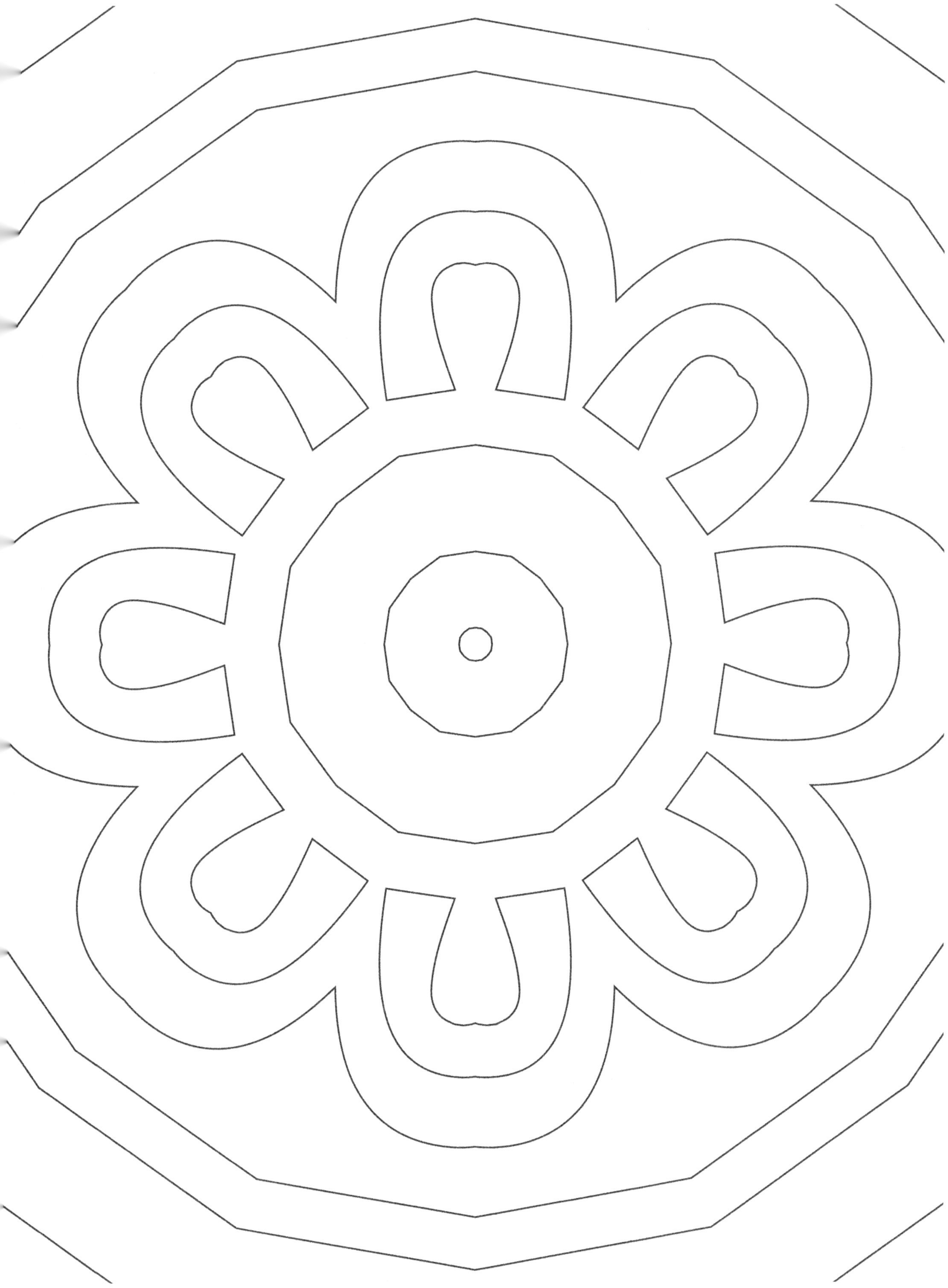

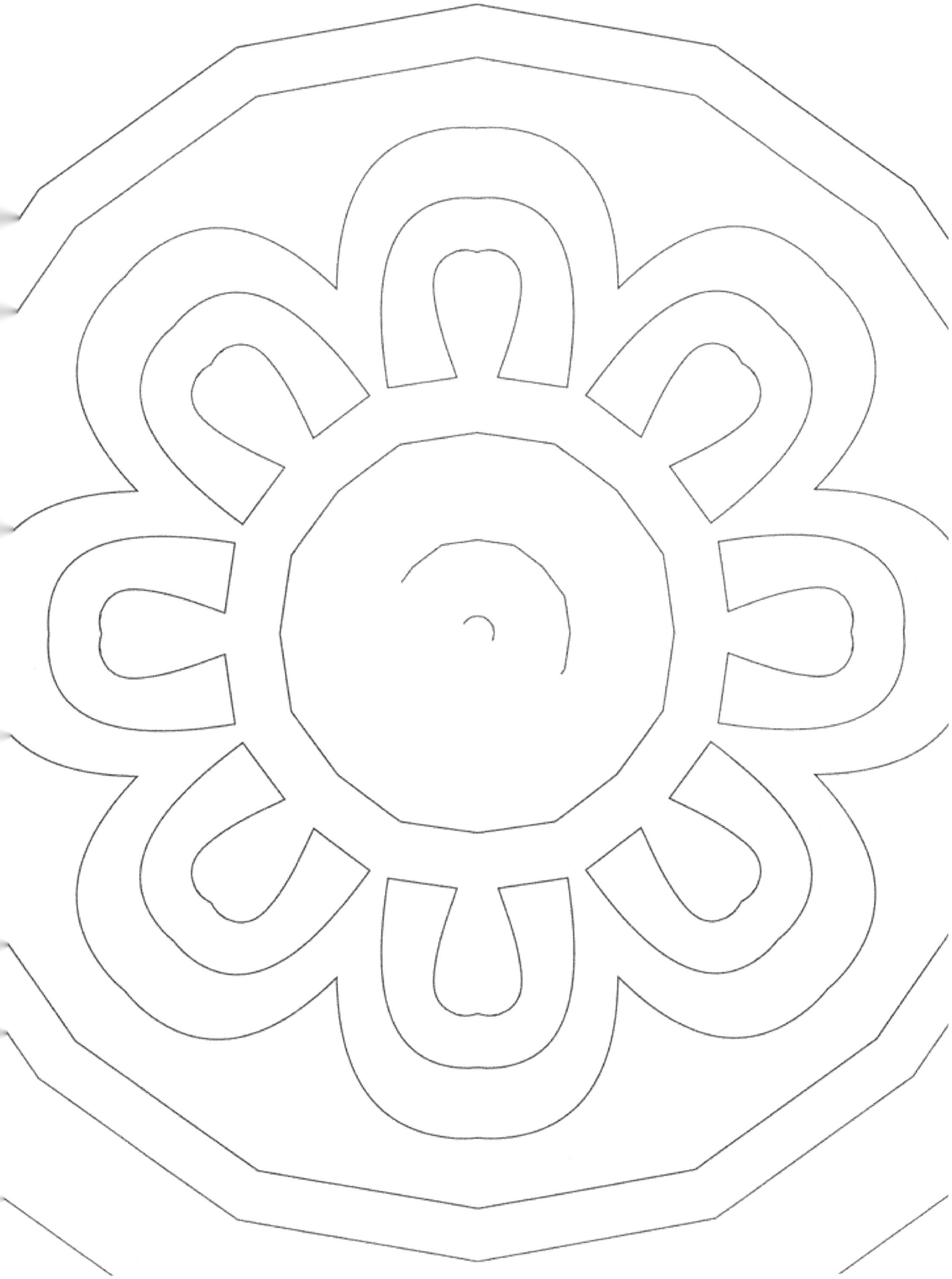

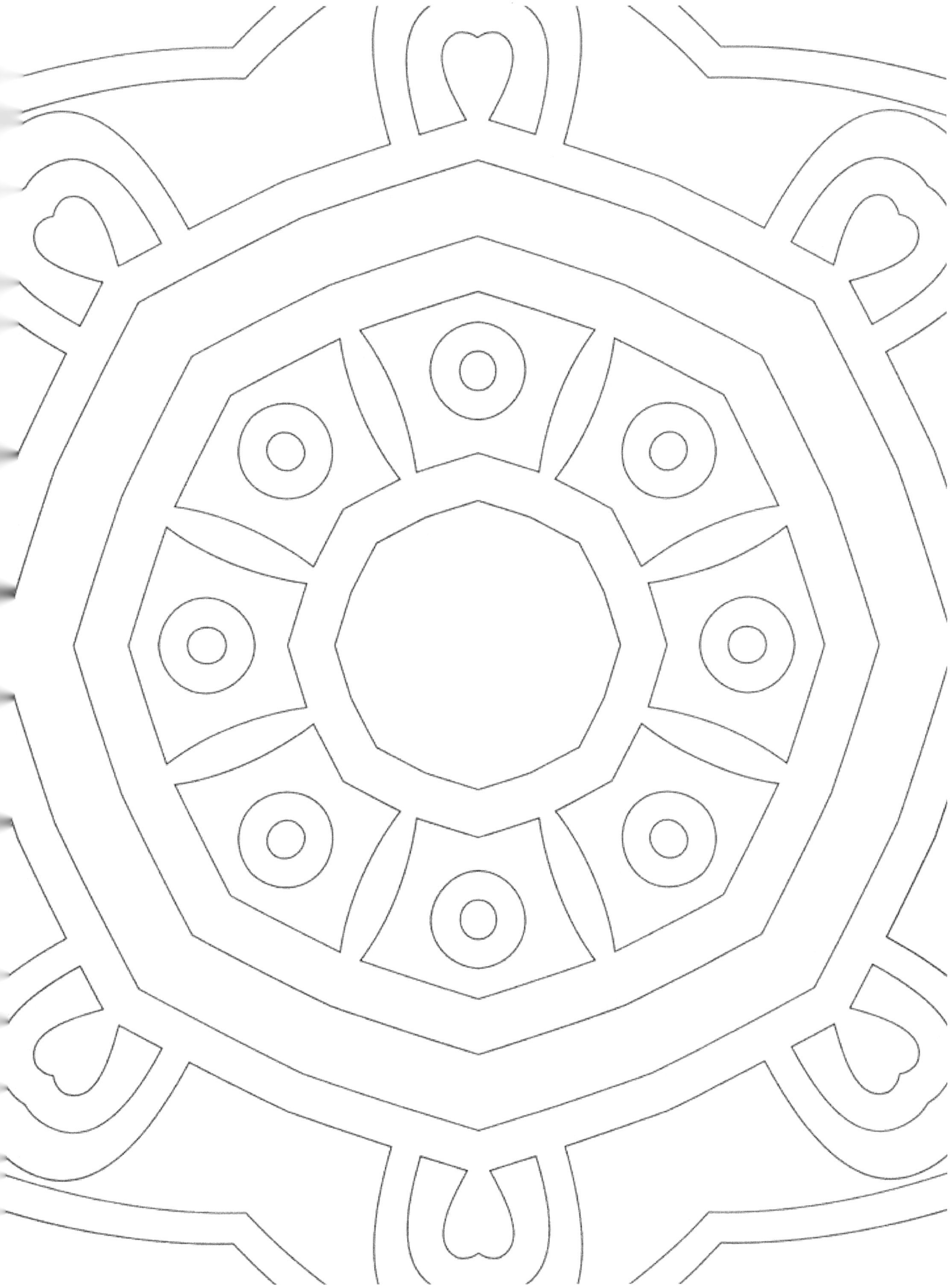

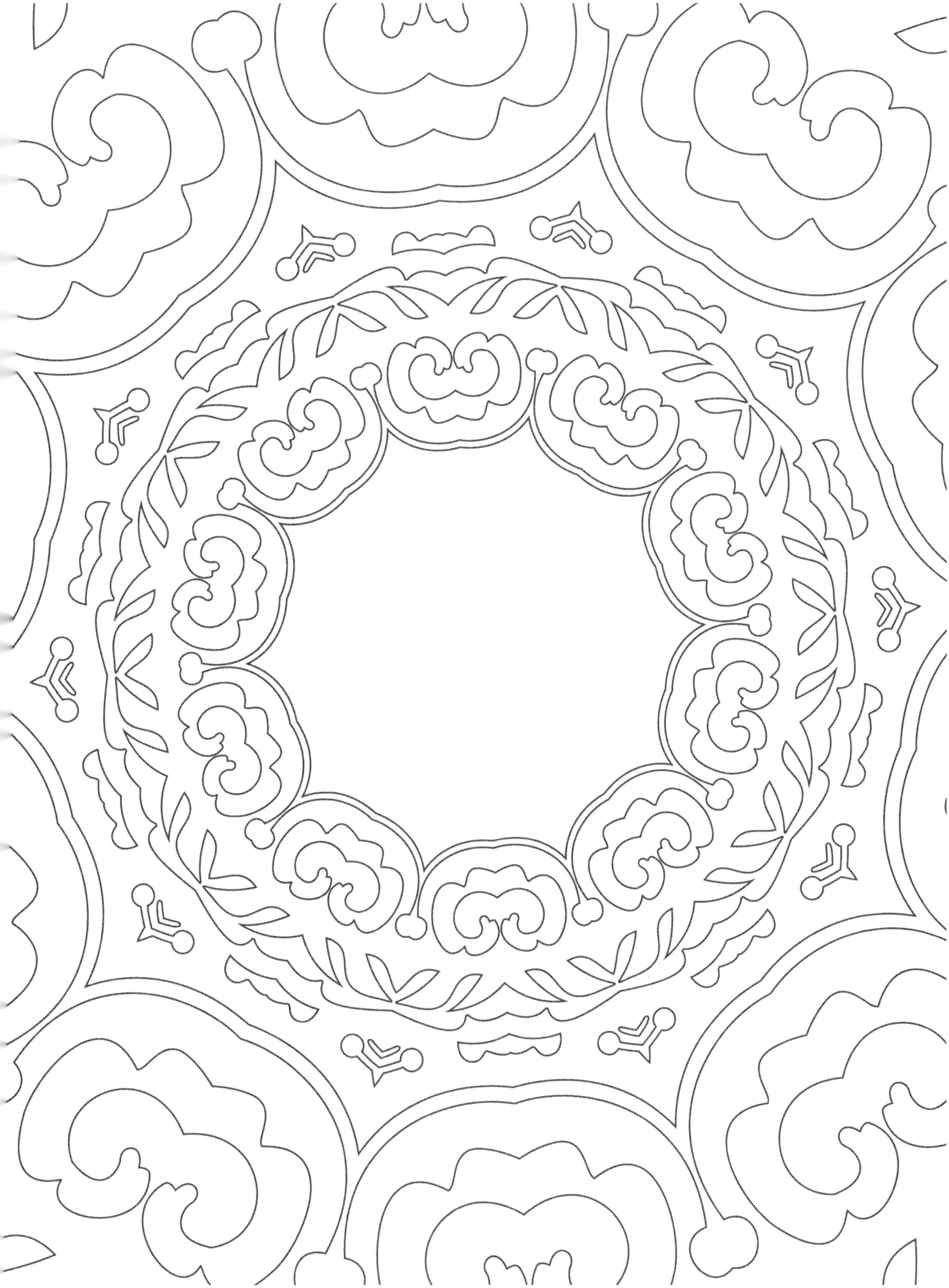

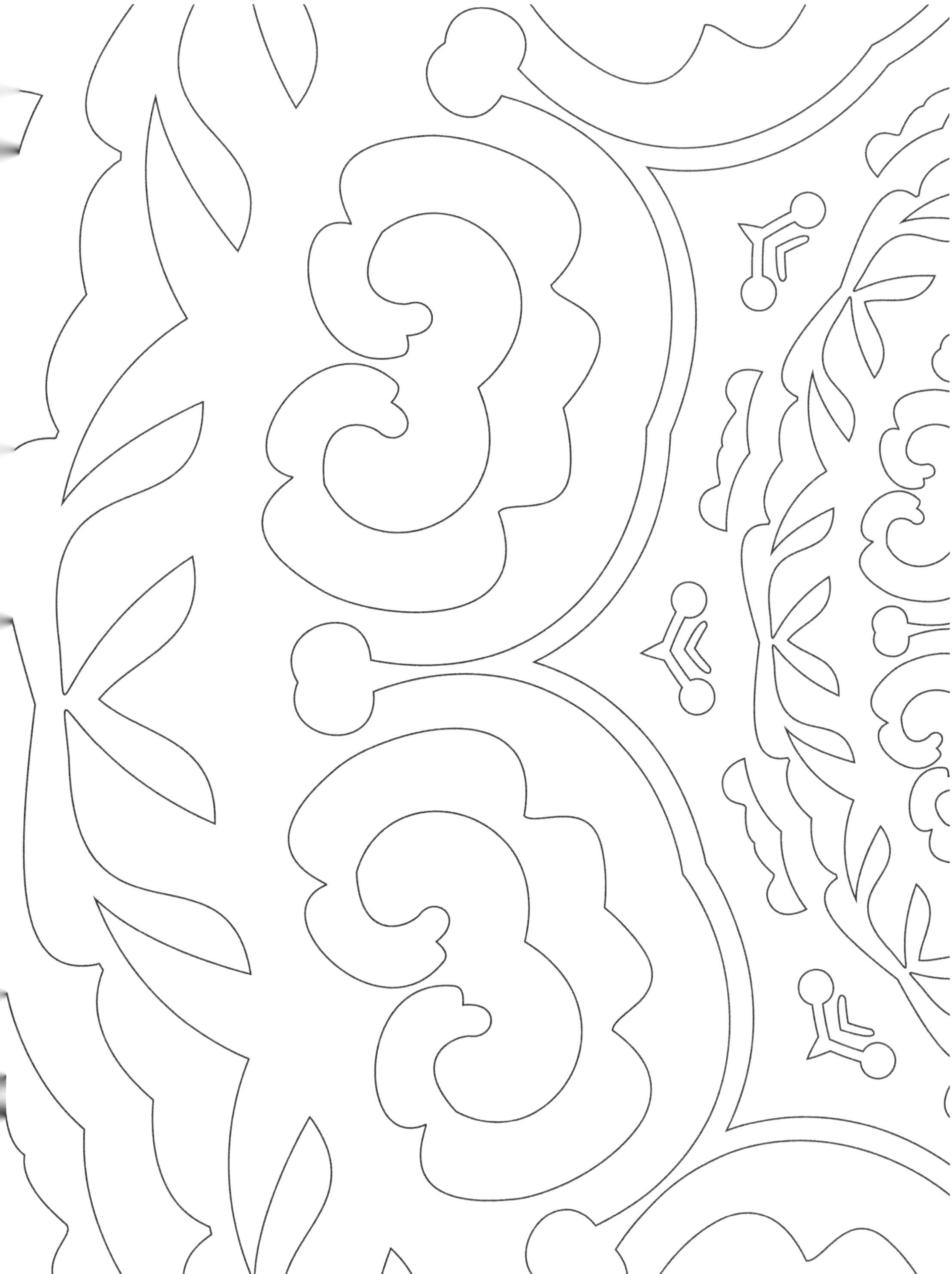

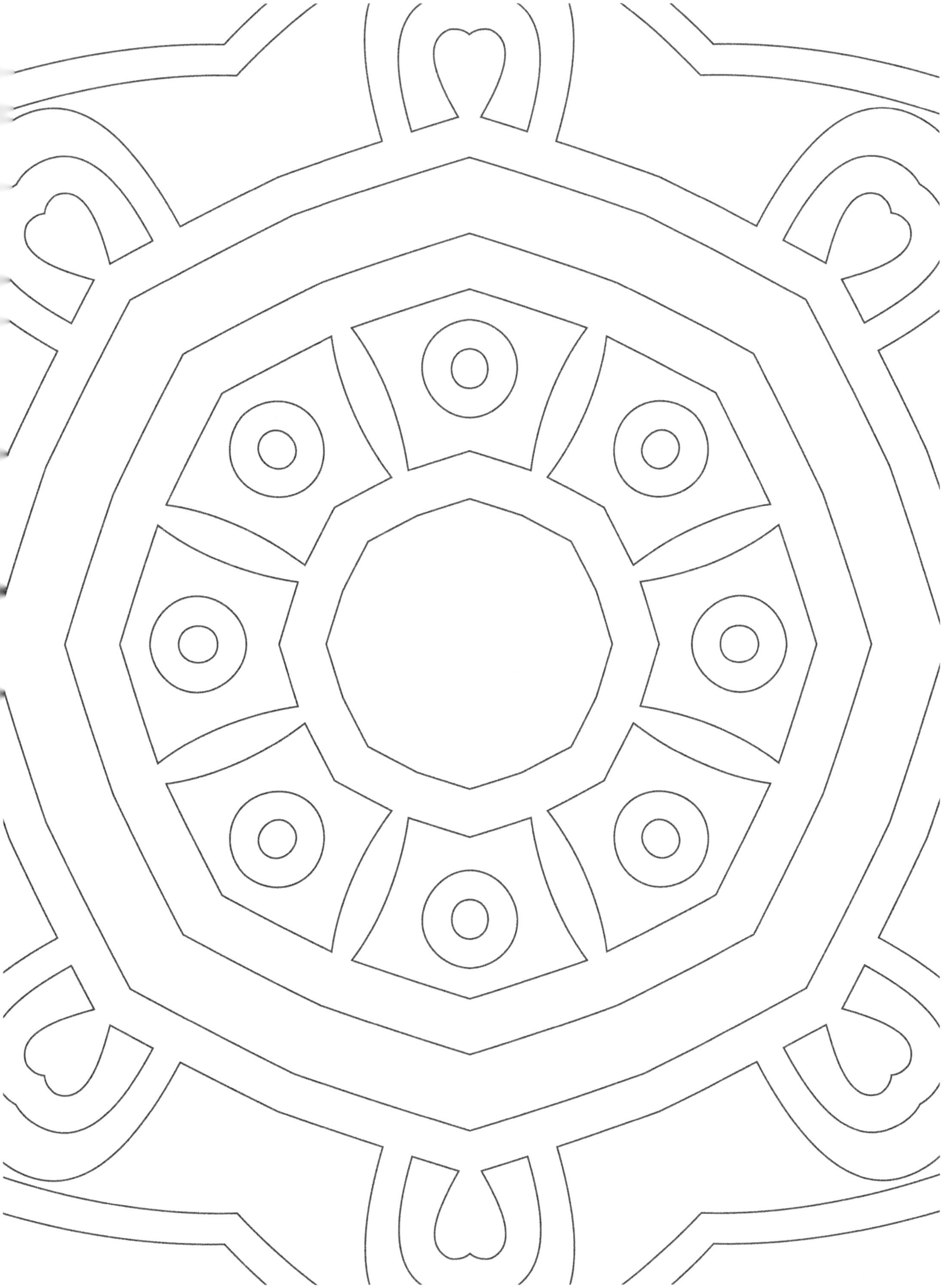

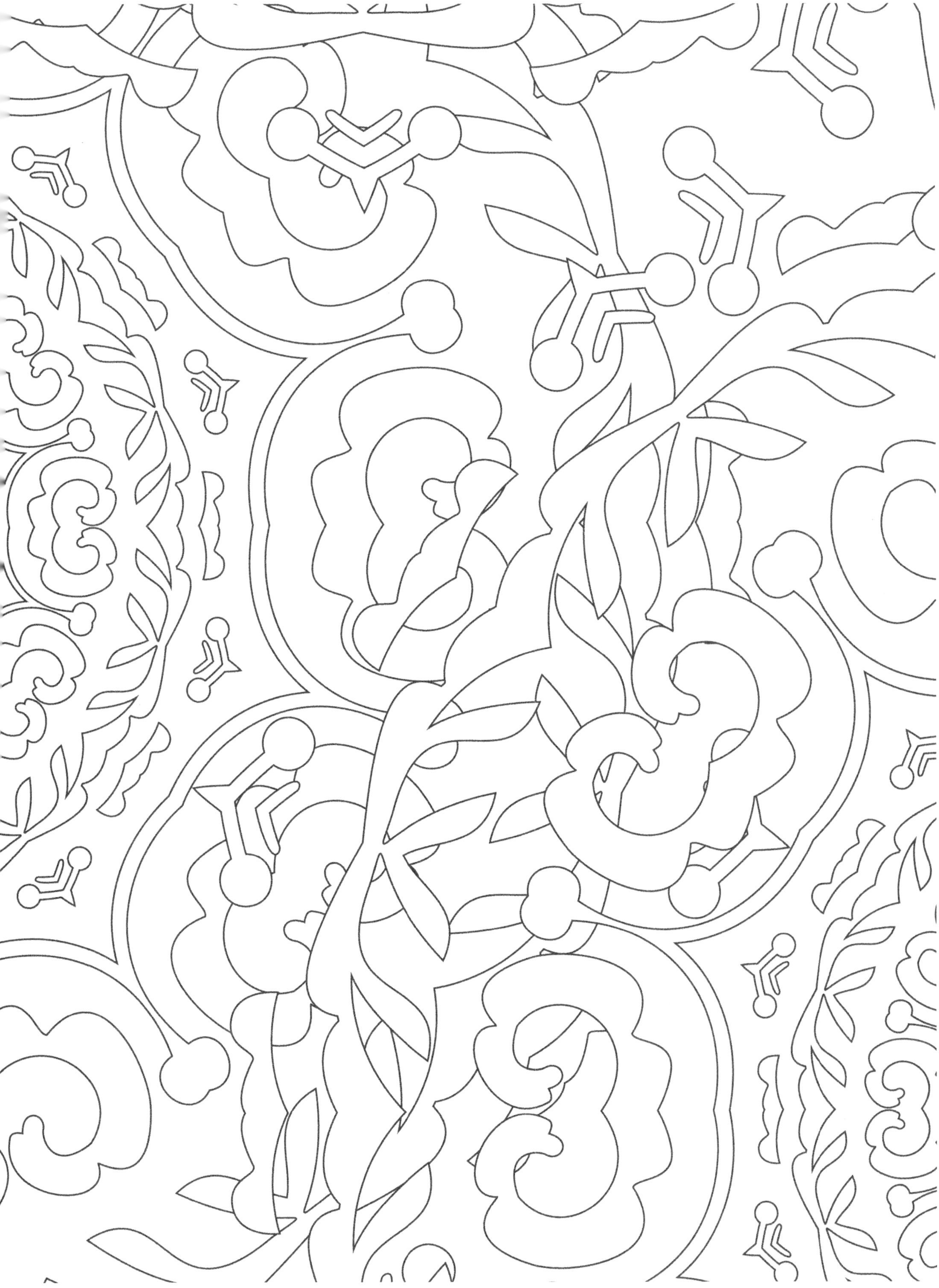

Made in the USA
Las Vegas, NV
13 December 2022

62348900R00066